CHRONICLES

of the

OUTER BANKS

CHRONICLES

of the

OUTER BANKS

FISH TALES AND SALTY GALES

SARAH DOWNING

Foreword by Matt Walker, *Outer Banks Milepost Magazine*

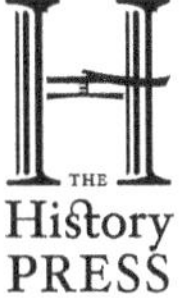

Published by The History Press
Charleston, SC
www.historypress.com

Front and back covers: *Color photos courtesy of Aycock Brown Collection, Outer Banks History Center; black-and-white photo courtesy of North Carolina Department of Conservation and Development Photo Collection, State Archives of North Carolina.*

First published 2019

Manufactured in the United States

ISBN 9781467140911

Library of Congress Control Number: 2018966263

CONTENTS

Contents

FOREWORD

Most everyone who falls in love with the Outer Banks does so by accident. A surf trip. A fishing weekend. A family vacation. A college job between semesters. For most, that's all it will ever be—a romantic summer fling with a stunning coastline. A stormy, passionate tryst full of cherished memories that linger forever. For others, the relationship becomes a lifelong love affair, where the more time you spend, the more you appreciate. Before long, scoring waves, gaffing fish and earning tips proves less rewarding than the bonds you make with your fellow beach addicts.

Stick around long enough—two consecutive winters according local lore—and you might find yourself so tangled up in the super-tight community that you find you can't leave. But if you mean to stay, you best be willing to work hard. Surviving here means giving it your all. Sacrificing for others. Working together to stay afloat. Do that, and you can't help but leave some sort of mark.

Perhaps that's why such a tiny community claims such a robust history. In fact, our one hundred miles of coast might just boast more landmark achievements than any place of similar size. Roanoke Island's home to both America's first attempted English settlement—a.k.a. the Lost Colony—and a settlement for refugee slaves during the Civil War, known as the Freedmen's Colony. Notorious pirate Blackbeard made Ocracoke his second home. The Wright brothers made repeated visits to pioneer aviation. All follow a similar pattern of a discovering a place, then doing whatever it takes to survive. (Albeit with differing results.)

And while achievements may stand among our most noteworthy moments, they're hardly alone. Between the major events, local lore is littered with smaller, but compelling historical notes that show the same commitment to our gritty abode. Moments where a shared adversity turned into potential opportunity for our community to shine and help others in the process.

Like the way making ice changed the whole way folks could harvest fish—resulting in a multi-million-dollar commercial industry that sends bushels of seafood all over the world and keeps local families' pockets full.

Or the summer a visit from a royal princess that sparked a regal makeover for the small town of Manteo, prompting an economic boom for the quaint downtown.

Or the winter Mac Midgett paid tribute to the history of "wrecking" along the coast, by claiming salvage rights on a late-70s shipwreck and ended up starting his own successful business and political career.

Or any number of long-forgotten traditions—from sturgeon fishing to sweet potatoes to flattop cottages—that once defined our area and influenced our region, only to give way to newer, greater means of staying alive. The events may not make international headlines. The players are far from famous. But they fall into the time-tested tradition of local people making a difference for the place they love most.

It's a phenomenon so common—so collectively shared—it in inspired the concept for both a local magazine, *Milepost,* and its motto: "Stuck here on purpose." A proud statement that the people who live here are the ones who chart its course. And they're willing to suffer all its many challenges to stay put. Nasty weather. Near-isolation. Nonstop economic diversity. When I started that humble rag in 2011, I knew we'd want to dig into those tales. And after one visit to the Outer Banks History Center, it was clear who'd do the telling. Sarah Downing's love for her home of thirty years—not just its past, but its present and future—yielded the perfect combination of experience and passion. As a result, she culls the most interesting stories of real, local life. They may never ripple across the planet like the achievements of Sir Walter Raleigh or the Wright brothers. But they surely resonate with the people who have a passion for the Outer Banks. And every story is an opportunity to share and solidify that passion for any reader who loves this place—whether they live here or not.

—Matt Walker, Kill Devil Hills

INTRODUCTION AND ACKNOWLEDGEMENTS

Most articles in this book, or similar versions of them, were published previously, chiefly in *Milepost* magazine, but also in *My Outer Banks Home*, *Outer Banks Visitors Guide* and *Hatteras Monitor*. A revised and updated version of "The Dedication of the Virginia Dare Memorial Bridge" appears courtesy of the Friends of the Outer Banks History Center, State Archives of North Carolina. These works span the author's writing career from its earliest days to the present. Many people were helpful in providing photographs, permissions, tidbits of knowledge and contact information. Thank you!

Rob Crawford, Nags Head, North Carolina, friend

Matt Walker, Kill Devil Hills, North Carolina, colleague, friend and editor of *Outer Banks Milepost*

Jamie Lanier, friend and colleague, archives technician, National Park Service at Fort Raleigh

Eric McCrory, George W. Bush Presidential Library

Matthew Hanson, Franklin D. Roosevelt Presidential Library

Kim Andersen, colleague, State Archives of North Carolina, Raleigh, North Carolina

Ian Dunn, colleague, State Archives of North Carolina, Raleigh, North Carolina

Sara Brewer, National Archives and Records Administration, Atlanta, Georgia

Carolyn Morris, friend and former neighbor, town clerk, Town of Nags Head, North Carolina
John Ratzenberger, Nags Head, North Carolina, friend and mentor
Cecelia Winslow, Raleigh and Nags Head, North Carolina
Samantha Crisp, Outer Banks History Center, Manteo, North Carolina
Stuart Parks, Outer Banks History Center, Manteo, North Carolina
Jake Hays, librarian, *Virginian-Pilot* newspaper
Kate Jenkins, editor, The History Press
Mary Ann Williams, Three Dog Ink, publisher of *My Outer Banks Home* and others
Jeff Donohue, friend and colleague, *Outer Banks Visitors Guide*
Brent McKee, friend and colleague, the Living New Deal
Barbara Snowden, friend, colleague and mentor, Currituck County Historian, North Carolina Historical Commission
David Miller, friend, Roanoke Island Festival Park, Manteo, North Carolina
Eric Blevins, photographer, North Carolina Museum of History, Raleigh, North Carolina
William B. Ball, National Aeronautics and Space Administration
Bill Brown, colleague, registrar, State Archives of North Carolina, Raleigh, North Carolina
Drew C. Wilson, friend and photographer, *Wilson Times* newspaper, Wilson, North Carolina
Roger P. Meekins, friend and photographer, Roanoke Island, North Carolina
Jane Adkisson, Pack Memorial Library, Asheville, North Carolina
Linda Lau, Fairfax, Virginia
Sue Berry, Wanchese, North Carolina
Jason E. Tomberlin, colleague; head, Research and Instructional Services, Wilson Special Collections Library, University of North Carolina at Chapel Hill
Kim Sawyer, colleague, Roanoke Island Festival Park, Manteo, North Carolina
Barbara Hird, friend, Elizabeth R and Co.
lebame houston, friend and mentor, Elizabeth R and Co, and historian Roanoke Island Historical Association
Matt Whaley, Joyner Library, East Carolina University
Jennifer Daugherty, Joyner Library, East Carolina University
Dale Sauter, Joyner Library, East Carolina University

PART I

NATIVE FLAVOR

WORKING THE ROE

Forget "Crab Sloughs" and Soft Shells, Caviar Was the First Real Coastal Delicacy

Talk to me about caviar
They ain't nothing but fish eggs packed in a jar
I got a whole pond of big round trout
Fish eggs, what are they talking about?
—Eddy Arnold, "Richest Man in the World"

How do you like your eggs? Scrambled. Fried. Or sturgeon? At the end of the nineteenth century, the short-nosed and Atlantic variety of this prehistoric fish were in high demand among local fishermen—both for their roe and for their meat—who caught them in nets in the rivers of eastern North Carolina and just off the coast at Nags Head and Hatteras. According to an 1895 article in Edenton's *Fisherman and Farmer* newspaper, "Sturgeon fishing was first introduced to North Carolina waters by Captain A.T. Cain an old experienced fisherman who came here from Delaware." And though still a new venture at the turn of the century, harvesting the finny beasts was "rapidly becoming an industry of no small proportions."

Neither were the fish, which could range between 150 and 300 pounds on average. Furthermore, the 453-page epic *Fishes of North Carolina*—published in 1907 as volume two of the North Carolina Geological and Economic Survey—reported examples "that were 12 feet long and weighed over 500 pounds....Two fish caught at Hatteras in the spring of 1906 were 9 and 11 feet long," fitting sizes for an animal from the dinosaur era. *Coastwatch* magazine says the Atlantic sturgeon dates back

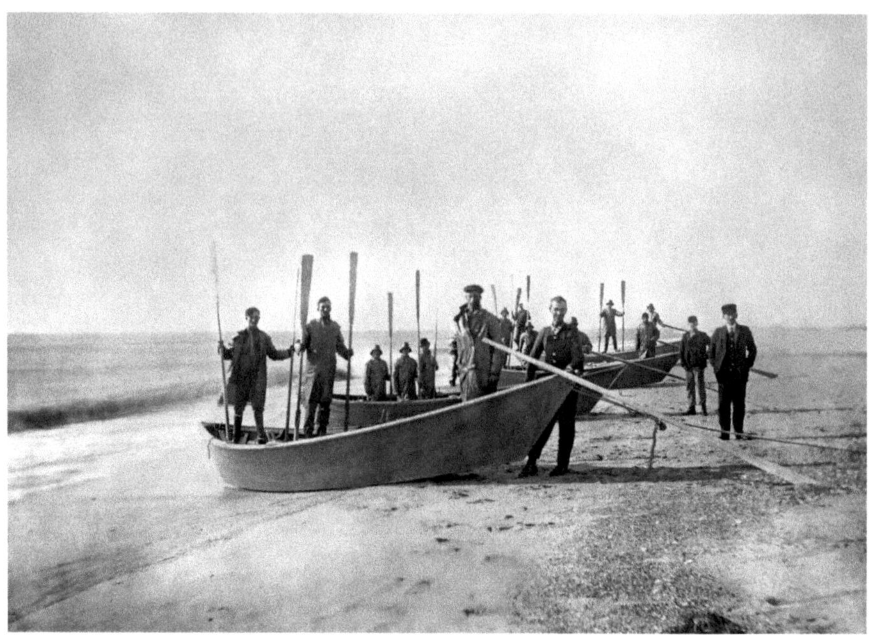

Fishermen and dories in Nags Head. At the time this photo was taken, Dare County led the state in sturgeon fishing. *Photo courtesy North Carolina Museum of History, 1905.*

120 million years and even has "dinosaur-like armor from five rows of bony plates, or scutes."

Needless to say, the fish wasn't pretty. But the insides were tasty—especially the eggs. So, every spring, fishermen went about setting cotton twine nets six hundred to one thousand feet long in the ocean, right about the time female "cows" swam upriver to spawn. A particularly precarious part of the ordeal was bringing in the fish alive. "They were no good if the fish had died in the net," noted Ernal Foster in a 1976 *Coastland Times* article written nearly forty years ago. (Captain Ernal, legendary charter boat captain and founder of the Albatross Fleet, was the son of Charles Foster and father of Ernie Foster, who continues the Hatteras Island fishing tradition.)

That meant moving fast. As soon as the egg-laden cows were brought back to shore, the roe (sometimes weighing as much as fifty to seventy-five pounds) was carefully extracted and then placed into a vat of brine until it became pliable. The next step was removing the membrane, known colloquially on Hatteras Island as "fleece." Fishermen placed the eggs into a large sieve and worked them through. These membrane-free eggs found their way into yet another tub of brine. Making the right solution was serious business: the brine had to be just salty enough to preserve and flavor the roe but not so salty that it would cook the delicate eggs. After preparers periodically tasted the solution to determine when the proper salinity had been achieved, the eggs were removed from the brine and placed on racks and left overnight. Finally, the prepared roe from four to six fish was packed into wooden kegs that fetched from twenty-five dollars to forty dollars.

They called this process "working the roe." And painstaking care was important at every step. "Otherwise," says Ernie Foster, "The eggs broke and you had nothing." In fact, the method of preparing the roe to make caviar was so guarded that Foster's father, Charlie, and another man performed the task in closed quarters so nobody else could learn the process. No wonder. By 1920, fish brokers from Philadelphia and New York were soliciting sturgeon caviar and meat in Elizabeth City's *Independent* newspaper.

Regrettably, when Foster died in 1953, he was the last man who knew how to "work the roe," and properly extract the black gold from the strange-looking fish and make it salable to markets in Europe. However, the industry continued a few decades longer. In 1974, commercial fishermen H.R. and Lee Craddock of Manns Harbor netted a 250-pound sturgeon laden with 30 pounds of roe, which fetched about seven dollars a pound.

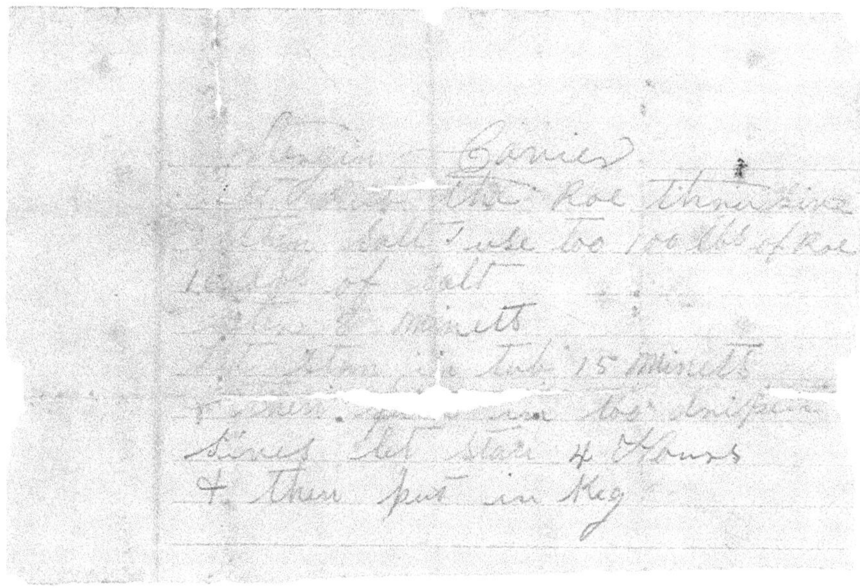

[illegible] Caviar
[illegible] the Roe [illegible]
[illegible] Salt I use too 100 lbs of Roe
[illegible] of Salt
[illegible] 8 minett
[illegible] in Tub 15 minetts
[illegible]
[illegible] 4 Hours
& Then put in Keg

An old handwritten recipe or receipt for sturgeon caviar, which calls for one hundred pounds of roe and sixteen pounds of salt. *PC 1184 Mrs. J. Emmett Winslow Collection, State Archives of North Carolina. Date unknown.*

Unfortunately, the fish populations couldn't keep pace with demand. In 1990, North Carolina yielded just seven thousand pounds of sturgeon. In 1991, the state placed protections on both the short-nosed and Atlantic sturgeon to preserve the remaining breeding stock. In 2012, the Carolina population of sturgeon was listed as endangered under the Endangered Species Act of 1973. But the prehistoric still fish still has its followers. Biologists, ichthyologists and fish specialists with the National Marine Fisheries service, North Carolina State University and the North Carolina Division of Marine Fisheries all monitor the sturgeon and collect data about the ancient aquatic animal to ensure its survival.

And caviar fans? Well, you can always satisfy your high-end tastes by ordering some Beluga caviar online—where an ounce will cost you one hundred dollars. Or you can just order the much more economical herring roe and eggs for breakfast.

THIS YAM IS YOUR YAM

How Captain Hayman Delivered a Sweet Holiday Tater

Did you know that North Carolina's state vegetable is the sweet potato? The Tar Heel State leads the nation in production of the root crop, and nothing ushers in the coming of autumn like buying a big box of them at a roadside stand or farmer's market. For less than twenty dollars, a carton will last through football get-togethers, pig pickins and other assorted seasonal pot lucks, carrying straight through Thanksgiving and the holidays and into the New Year. (Just make sure to stock up on marshmallows or coconut and pecans.)

But on the Outer Banks, one variety stands apart—the Hayman sweet potato. Known more locally as a Kill Devil Hills beach access or public park, the name's first claim to fame is as a tasty tuber, first brought to the East Coast by a local captain before making its way into recipes and pies farther north.

"On the Eastern Shore they are kind of a well-kept secret," says Lorraine Eaton, staff epicure at the *Virginian-Pilot* newspaper. "They love their Hayman sweet potatoes."

Sweet potatoes (there are scores of varieties) are thought to have originated in Central and South America. The tuber was growing when Christopher Columbus came poking around the New World, and he took samples back to Spain. Portuguese traders introduced the sweet potato to West Africa. The root crop spread eastward to Asia, but also made its way westward from Peru to Polynesia and New Zealand.

By 1648, historical records show Virginia farmers cultivating sweet potatoes; by 1723, they had made their way to Carolina, where they remained an important food source feeding Americans in the colonial period, the Revolutionary and Civil Wars and on through the Great Depression.

But the introduction of the Hayman sweet potato— also referred to as the Hayman potato—dates back to 1859. That's when Captain Daniel Hayman sailed the schooner *Sally Smith* through Hatteras Inlet up the sounds and along the Pasquotank River to Elizabeth City with a barrel of yams—a batch of white sweet potatoes he had brought from the West Indies. The event was recorded by John Rollinson, Frisco resident, Hatteras Island native and journal keeper, who was at that time collector of revenue for the Port of Hatteras. (Other goods Hayman carried were three puncheons of molasses, three barrels of molasses, nine hundred oranges, four bottles of gin and a barrel of sugar.)

Now, Cap'n Hayman was a seafaring man, as were his neighbors Willis Partridge, Bird Beasley and his brother Matthias Hayman. He made his home near Kitty Hawk when he wasn't sailing between the Outer Banks and the Caribbean. When he was back in port, Cap'n Hayman made up for his time at sea by planting seeds of a different sort. (A blurb in Elizabeth City's *Economist and Falcon* newspaper printed just months before his death in September 1891 claimed he fathered more than thirty children between two wives.) But the sweet potato that bears his name remains his most celebrated offspring.

C.W. Hollowell of Bayside Plantation, south of Elizabeth City, and later owner of the Nags Head Hotel, described the tuber's virtue for the *Farmer and Mechanic* newspaper in 1877: "We consider it quite an acquisition to our potato crop, as we have less trouble in getting the sprouts to live when set out than any other variety we have here. They grow rapidly, mature early, and will afford more food for hogs than any crop I can plant on the same ground."

While we usually think of sweet potatoes as orange in color, the Hayman sweet potato has white skin and a creamy flesh that can appear grayish to greenish when raw. It was grown locally for a number of years and could be found in markets in the Albemarle area, Raleigh and Norfolk. In fact, in 1919, Joe Tom Daniels of Wanchese reportedly grew one nearly three feet in length.

But almost as soon as the Hayman sweet potato found its way to North Carolina, it was destined for a new market. A traveling Methodist minister (they were known to take advantage of maritime routes) came into possession

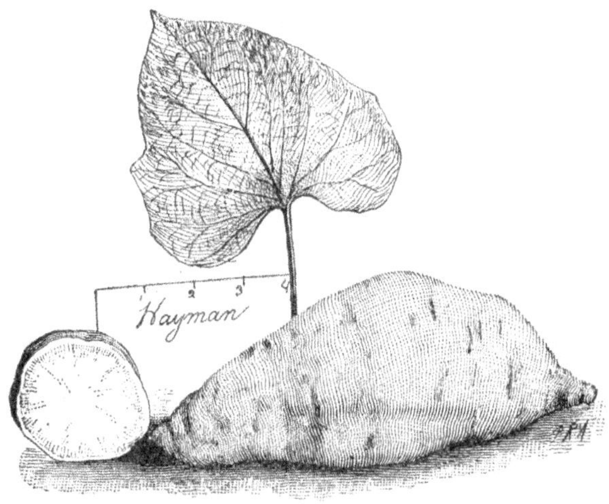

Artist rendering of a Hayman sweet potato. *From* Sweet Potato Culture for Profit: A Full Account of the Origin, History and Botanical Characteristics of the Sweet Potato *by Robert Henderson Price, 1896.*

of the first batch of Hayman taters, and he transported some to the Eastern Shore, the sliver of Maryland and Virginia separated from the mainland by the Chesapeake Bay.

While researching over the years, Eaton has come across many old handwritten recipes using the heirloom Haymans. She says outside of the Delmarva peninsula they aren't very well known, but they remain an autumn tradition along the Eastern Shore.

"People usually buy them by the box," she explained. "They need to cure a while and people say they should be eaten by St. Patrick's Day. They are a funny potato."

CALL OF THE CURRITUCKERS

Currituck County, North Carolina's northernmost political division, is a marsh lover's dream. The western mainland is separated from the Currituck Banks by the brackish Currituck Sound, which is fringed with wetlands and dotted with scores of islands—Knotts, Churches, Bells, Monkey and Swan for a start. The name *Currituck*, in fact, derives from an Algonquian word meaning "land of the wild goose," and for a time in the 1980s, Curritucckers were champion goose callers on the state and national levels.

Even before the Civil War, the area attracted the eyes of sportsmen interested in coming down to hunt waterfowl that were drawn to Currituck's bays and marshes by the millions. Although the Currituck Hunt Club was established in 1857, hunting or shooting clubs began to flourish following the War Between the States. Union soldiers returned home carrying with them stories of the area's abundant ducks, geese and swan, which overwintered in Currituck Sound, an important stop along the migratory route known as the Atlantic flyway. Clubs ranged from the opulent to the understated and varied in membership, size and accommodations. As they were established, so were jobs for local residents. Men and occasionally women were employed as caretakers, guides and cooks.

Currituck native Erleen Gallop Snow (1919–1990) was brought up with this waterfowl heritage. She was a three-time state champion goose caller, winning consecutive titles starting in 1985 at the Currituck Wildlife Festival. She also placed second three years in a row at the World Goose Calling

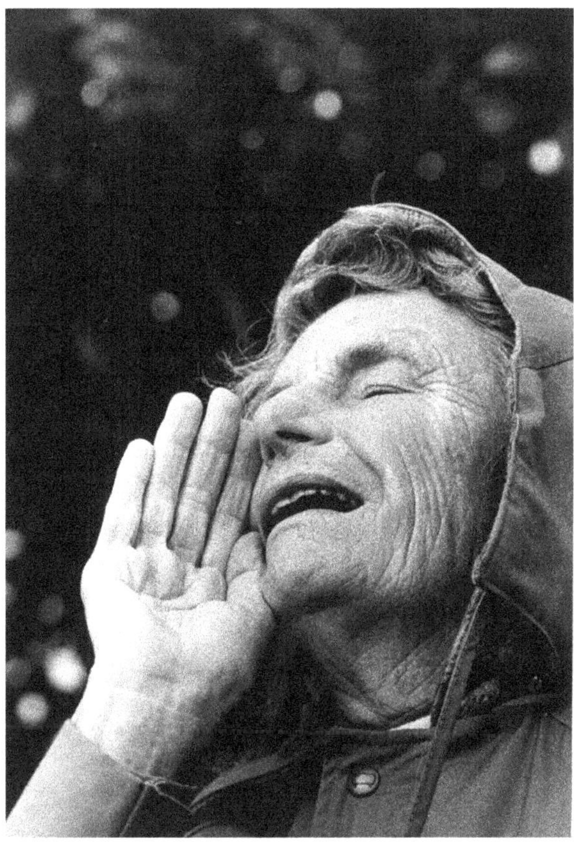

Erleen Snow of Currituck County demonstrates her method of calling geese, which won her a state title. Snow used her voice and not a wooden or plastic call. *Drew C. Wilson Collection, Outer Banks History* Center, *1988.*

Championships held each year at the Waterfowl Festival in Easton on Maryland's Eastern Shore.

In native fashion, Mrs. Snow did not use a wooden or plastic call when calling geese: Erleen just used her voice, otherwise known as voice calling. She learned the skill from her father, a fisherman and later a hunting guide, Erwin Gallop.

"That was always the norm for Currituck Sound," explained Bill Privott. "Voice calling was natural." And he should know. Privott clenched the World Goose Calling title in 1983 and 1984, competing against challengers who used "devices" to make their calls. "The first year I won I was the only voice caller," a fact he is pleased to share.

During a competition, contestants give four distinct calls—and you thought they just let out a honk or two! Contestants must give a hail call, a greeting call, a comeback call and a confidence call. All are different forms of goose-talk.

Privott was raised in Currituck. "I grew up right there on what is now courthouse road." He says that he showed an interest in wildfowl early on. A family story passed down attests to the fact—he would stand by the window and talk to the birds. "They tell me I started calling geese at three years old," he recollected. "It was like decoy carving in those days, like a folk art."

"I can call geese better when I see geese. It's like a shot of adrenaline," Privott divulged. In his younger days, he hunted and also served as a guide for twelve years. "So, practice came from practical experience in the field." Privott's son, Brad, was raised with the tradition as well and also started calling at an early age. In 1993, he won the Junior Championship using a call, but in 1996, he opted to compete with his voice. Brad made a good decision, because he cinched the competition and was awarded the title a second time.

So, what happens after one earns goose calling accolades? Well, in 1988, Erleen was recorded by the Smithsonian Institution to be made part of its permanent archives. She appeared on the *Today* show and was interviewed by John Albert. She has been described as "a national heroine."

Bill and Brad Privott were filmed on location at Bell's Island in Currituck, where they talked with Harry Smith for the television program *CBS This Morning*. Additionally, Brad Privott appeared on both *The David Letterman Show* and *The Jerry Springer Show*, in an episode his father contends "was the only show fit to watch, it had a bunch of kids with unusual talents."

Bill is concerned with the fate of the Canada goose, whose calls he mimicked. They have become comfortable inhabiting settled areas with man-made ponds such as parks and golf courses and in some cases no longer migrate. According to Privott, "Only about ten percent have retained any homing instinct."

After retiring from a thirty-four-year career as a Currituck County magistrate, Bill now spends his working days at the Bells Island Campground, a recreational oasis on the Currituck Sound that has been in his wife's family for fifty-five years.

CRIMSON INCOME

Inner Bankers, Cranberries and Supplemental Cash at the Turn of the Last Century

The marshes and swampy lowlands that border the Outer Banks are rich with history, culture and biodiversity. In fact, the terrain is home to one tart treasure that for years helped inhabitants of mainland Dare and nearby counties supplement their seasonal fishing incomes: wild cranberries (aka *Varccinium macrocarpon).*

This creeping shrub thrives in boggy ecosystems like the low-lying areas of northeastern North Carolina. At the turn of the twentieth century, collecting cranberries was a means as viable as hunting or fishing for natives to provide for their families. Before mechanization and modern processing, collecting berries for market was profitable for those living in the mainland enclaves of Manns Harbor, Mashoes, Stumpy Point and Gum Neck.

Foragers used large wooden rakes, often passed down from one generation to the next, to harvest the crimson gems from the swampy bogs. According to Outer Banks writer, photographer, publicity man and keeper of history Aycock Brown, the rakes were "box-like in shape with the bottom having many wooden prongs which separate the berries from the multi-leaf cranberry plant."

In 1901, state engineer J.H. McRee came upon a three-thousand-acre cranberry bog while surveying a section of Tyrrell County. By the time he finished his assessment of the swamplands, McRee had discovered even more fruity patches described as full of berries which old timers said "were not planted, but have always been there."

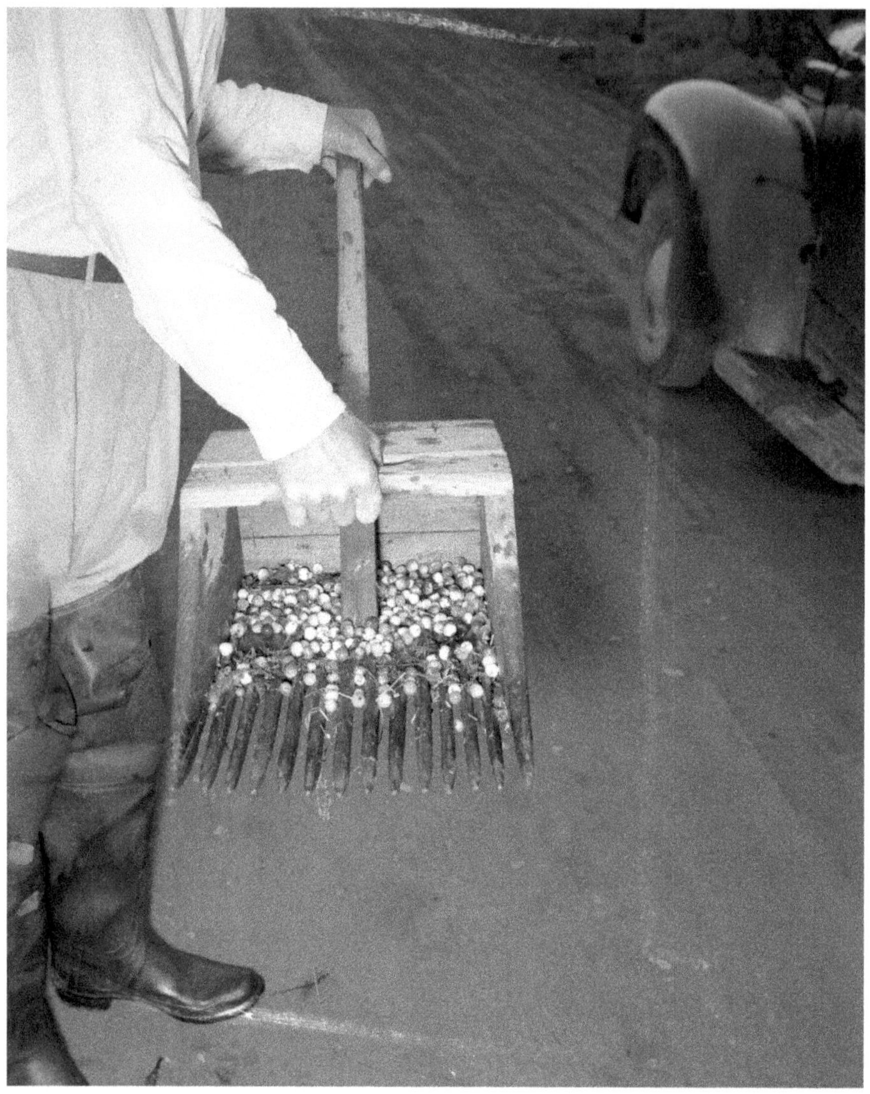

Large wooden rakes, often passed from one generation to the next, were used to collect cranberries from marshy areas of Dare, Currituck and Tyrrell Counties. *North Carolina Department of Conservation and Development Photo Collection, State Archives of North Carolina, 1947.*

In some cases, there was more supply than they could actively harvest. Raleigh's *Farmer and Mechanic* newspaper attested to the abundance of wild-growing fruit in the area in 1907. But, while the soil in North Carolina's northeast coastal section was well suited to raising berries, there were no appropriate means to get the crops to market:

> *There are extensive cranberry marshes within five miles of this place (Columbia), one of the finest being near the headwaters of Riders Creek. Other marshes are found in Hyde and Tyrrell counties, and still another (reported as producing an extra fine berry) is an island near the mouth of Northwest River in Currituck County. Also the fruit grows in a wild state on a stretch of land bordering the Croatan Sound in Dare County.*
>
> *These cranberry areas have never been cultivated; in fact, very little attention has been given them, mainly for the lack, up to a few months ago, of railroad facilities, and the further reason that the ownership of the land is in many instances unsettled. Otherwise it might be made a very profitable business, as the lands here are of that rich, peaty nature peculiarly adapted to the growth of cranberries.*

None of this information was new to New England growers who wanted in on the southern berry action. As early as 1896, prominent Massachusetts cranberry man Captain C.W. Chase made his way to Elizabeth City, where he purchased tracts along the Pasquotank River. Chase cited North Carolina's earlier growing season, inexpensive land and cheaper labor as chief reasons for purchasing land in the northern Albemarle region where the berries grew naturally.

In 1907, Dare County's crop went down in the annals of history when Roanoke Island man-about-town and North Carolina fisheries commissioner Theodore Meekins Sr. entered some local wild cranberries in the horticulture exhibits at the Jamestown Exposition. Meekins's berries won a bronze medal, which he kept in his Manteo office, but it was lost in the great fire of September 1939.

By 1952, Thomas Hunter Midgett was one of the few natives still gathering cranberries the way his family had done for years, with the same wooden rake that his grandfather used, according to an article in the *Coastland Times*. Midgett grew up in Manns Harbor and courted Leona Basnight, whose parents were caretakers of the Durant's Island Hunt Club, located in the Albemarle Sound just north of the Dare County mainland. According to his daughter, Mary Alice Twiddy, Midgett would take a boat to call on her mother. "That was love, wasn't it," she said recently of her parent's watery courtship.

When interviewed in 1951, Midgett touted local berries over commercial ones for their taste and nutrients, "Still those cultivated berries in pretty packages do not have the taste, the size nor the quality of our wild berries." Twiddy and her brother recall their father collecting cranberries, saying

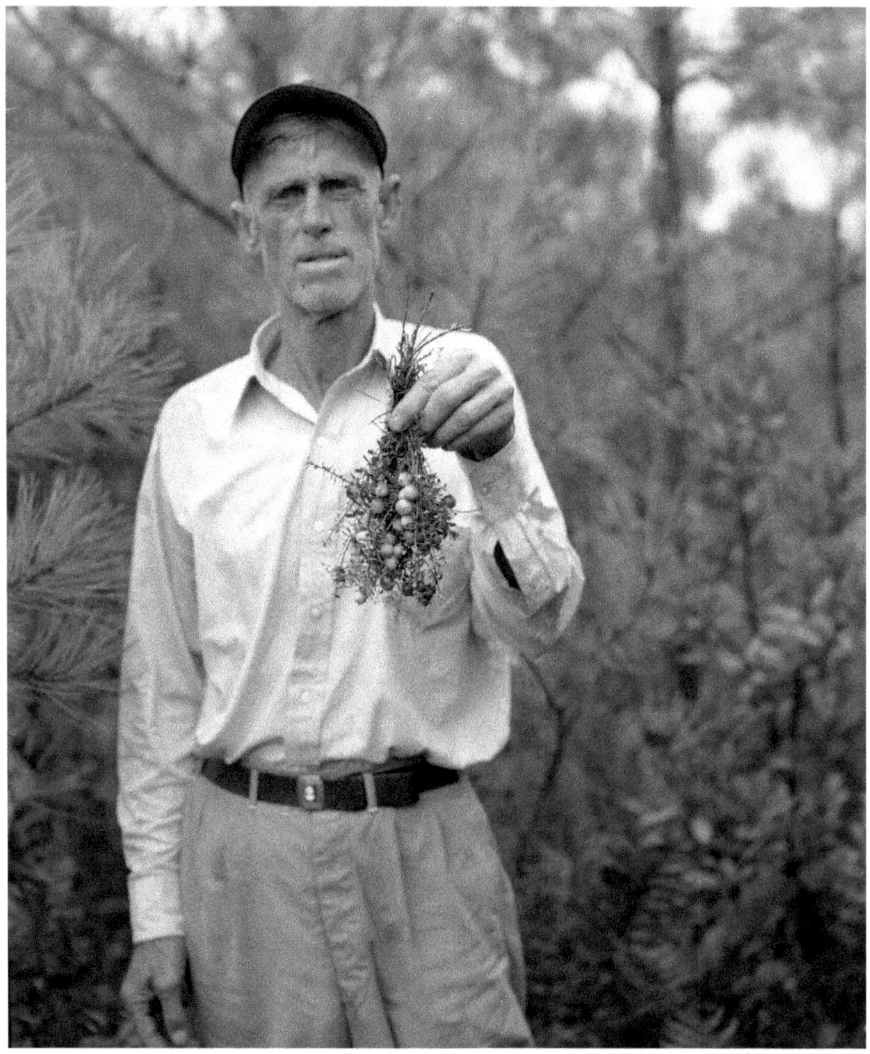

Prior to commercial production, collecting wild cranberries was a reliable supplementary income for mainlanders, such as this Stumpy Point gent. *North Carolina Department of Conservation and Development Photo Collection, State Archives of North Carolina, 1947.*

"they went up Mashoes Road in the fall." When asked if she had seen her father's wooden cranberry rake, Twiddy was quick to respond, "I sure did"; however, the longtime Manns Harbor resident was not sure of its whereabouts. "I don't know where it would be," she regretted.

Perhaps it merely fell to the wayside, like many of the old hunting and gathering traditions of our forebearers.

CONFESSIONS FROM A SMALL TOWN

Although Spread Out, the Outer Banks Can Be Right Neighborly

I'll never forget, shortly after moving to the Outer Banks, realizing the need to shed my big-city ways. I was at the electric company paying a bill, and for some reason I was not polite to the woman at the counter. Perhaps I was still in my city mode—rush, rush, rush—and the cashier was moving at a pace not up to my expectations. I spouted out a caustic comment, not thinking I'd ever see her again. Much to my surprise, there she was the next time I visited the office. And the time following, and the time after that too. Label me rude. I deserved it.

I discovered I was living in a small town, or at least along a thin stretch of sand made up of small towns, and I would see the same people day in and day out. Long gone were impersonal interactions with folks with whom I'd never again cross paths. I began to slow down and see everything with a new perspective. The people with whom I came in contact each day were friends and neighbors, and together we were all part of a caring community.

Oh sure, sometimes we wish we could run our list of errands to the bank, the hardware store, the gas station, and not have to schedule extra time for visiting. On a recent trip to the grocery store, I threw my hand up to greet friends waiting in the checkout line. Exiting the store, I ran into another friend and colleague. We stopped, chitchatted, and she complimented my new dress and I admired her new car, which she pointed out across the parking lot. Then walking to my vehicle, I shared a quick kiss with another friend, who barely broke stride but admonished me in her southern drawl, "When are we gonna do lunch?" But for the most part, these commonplace meetings are the threads that weave us together and make us strong.

After moving to Nags Head from the Greater Pittsburgh area in 1999, Don and Rose Talmadge were quick to notice the friendly nature of their new hometown. "We'd walk down the Beach Road…everybody waved at you, no matter what," Don recollected. "I didn't matter if you knew them."

As the lumberyard manager at Kellogg Building Supply in Manteo, Talmadge was quickly immersed in the local community and enjoyed getting to know new people. He was particularly struck by their easygoing and down-home ways. "When I moved here, Rose thought I was repeating myself. I would come home and say I met the nicest person I ever met, and then I would come home the next day and say I met the nicest person I ever met. She would say, yeah, you told me yesterday, but I'd say, no, this is somebody new."

The nurturing characteristics of a small community often arise in times of need. After a medical emergency, Talmadge remembers how friends stepped in to help him out of a bind. "I had torn the siding off my house. We put a new deck on, and then I end up with a blood clot and in the hospital for ten days or two weeks. I had no siding on the house and Steve and Big Bob came over and put siding on the house."

Marty Saunders, of Kill Devil Hills, raised her three children on the Outer Banks, and even gave birth to her youngest at home. "It was a very good place to have a family," she said. "I loved knowing lots of people doing what you do with kids. Schools, and sports and dance recitals and Girls Scouts and surfing and skimming." Her west-side neighborhood, First Flight Village, is home to many year-round families, and as such has been known for many years as *the* place for trick-or-treaters. "It's the mob scene at Halloween," Saunders laughed. "It's crazy."

When her children were young, Marty met other young mothers in her neighborhood and at story hour at the Manteo Library. She forged strong friendships which exist to this day. "It was amazing the people I met and I still know," she said. When it was time to make the decision about giving birth at home, Saunders knew she could rely on these friends. "I wasn't afraid to do things like that because I felt like there were people here that I knew that would help me, would support me, that didn't look at me like I was crazy doing what I was doing."

Now an empty nester, Marty is contemplating continuing her education, and like many local residents is looking at online options for graduate coursework. "When I first lived here you knew you were going to have to travel somewhere to learn something else," she recalls. "Now I know lots of people who have done their masters degrees here and have never left Dare County to do it." These distance degree programs allow for options that were once only available in large university towns.

Shea Foreman was born in nearby Elizabeth City. Other than attending college in the North Carolina mountains, he has always called Kitty Hawk home. Foreman works at his family's business, the Sea Kove Motel. Shea recalls as a youngster in Kitty Hawk, he often played with the children of hotel guests, "I always had a pool and the beach, and lots of kids." He doesn't think he missed out anything by not living in a traditional neighborhood. Shea especially cherishes the wide-open spaces of his hometown and the natural areas of the Outer Banks. "You can find places where there aren't any people, at all, and I feel like that's rare in so many places."

Growing up, he attended Kitty Hawk Elementary, First Flight Middle and Manteo High Schools, and still maintains relationships with classmates. "We don't think we really need to do a high school reunion, because we have one

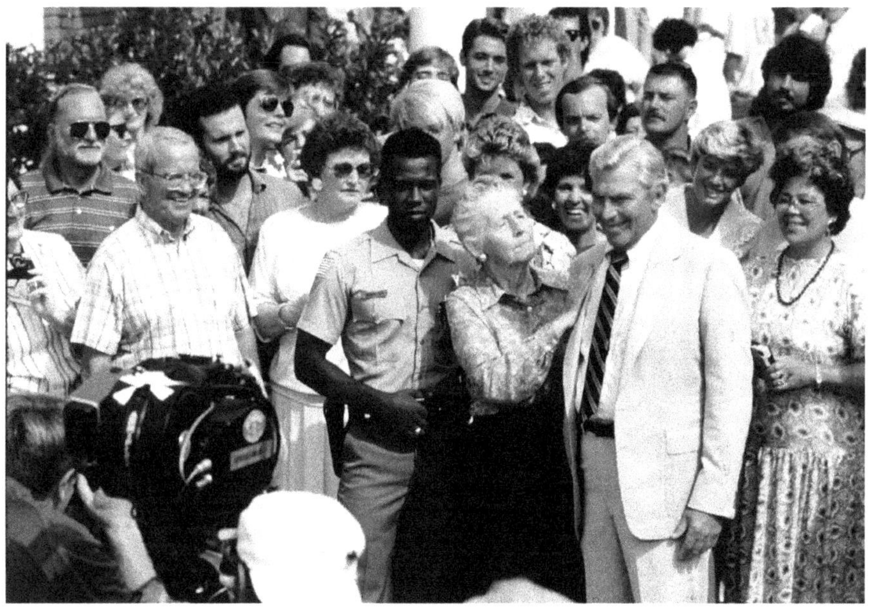

Manteo or Mayberry? Andy Griffith *(second from right)* is surrounded by natives and locals in downtown Manteo during the filming of an episode of *Matlock*. Griffith, a North Carolina native, performed in the outdoor drama *The Lost Colony* in the late 1940s, and later owned a home on Roanoke Island. The area's small-town charm was the perfect backdrop for the two-hour season premiere. *Drew C. Wilson photograph. Collection of the photographer, 1989.*

every day," he says with a smile. Frequently, Shea will also run into former teachers around town.

"It would drive a lot of people crazy, but I like seeing the same people all the time," Foreman explains. "I don't mind that. I feel like in a huge city it takes a lot to be known, you know, you have to work harder at it. Here, with the smallest effort, you can know everyone and it's not hard at all."

Intimacy, community spirit and a sense of belonging are some of the many things Outer Bankers, native and newcomer, list as reasons they find the area such a comfortable place to call home. Knowing your neighbors and being friendly with the girl at the convenience store or the fellow at the gas station are all part of the everyday existence here that lend to its small-town charm.

It's been over twenty-five years since I was rude to the lady at the electric company, but I still feel bad about it. Since that time, I learned to slow down and to wave. I mastered the art of chitchat. I smile and greet people on the street, in the checkout line at the store or on the beach.

I know twenty-five years is a long time. Bettie, I'm sorry.

PART II

BOUNTEOUS WATERS

SEA B&B

How the Croatan *Went from State Vessel to State of Vacation*

"Summer rental. Sleeps four. $300 per week...." Sound too good to be true? That's just for starters. Thirty years ago, this vacation opportunity wasn't just a killer bargain—it was a dry-docked vessel turned hospitality suite, the latest in many one-of-a-kind experiences for a former North Carolina state fisheries boat named *Croatan*.

From the beginning, the *Croatan* was special. It was born at New Bern's legendary Barbour Boatworks, a cradle of quality workboats between the 1930s and 1970s—if a boat was Barbour-built, that was the equivalent of a Thoroughbred horse, Tiffany glass, Tanqueray. On March 9, 1939, she was christened on a cold day at the state port docks in Morehead City, when, in true down-east Carteret County style, Beaufort's Catharine O'Bryan broke a bottle of clam juice across its graceful bow surrounded by members of the North Carolina Department of Conservation and Development.

From there, the forty-foot diesel-powered *Croatan* joined an eight-vessel state fleet. Larger boats kept watch offshore for fisheries violations—such as net limits and fishing out of season—while smaller boats like *Croatan* guarded the sounds. (In fact, Roanoke Island's Tom Basnight, who was assistant fisheries commissioner for a quarter century, also served as *Croatan*'s captain for a number of years.)

"These boats are used in patrolling our waters to enforce our rules and regulations, to collect taxes and licenses and to occasionally do experimental work," states the *Biennial Report of the North Carolina Department of Conservation and Development* for the period ending June 30, 1940.

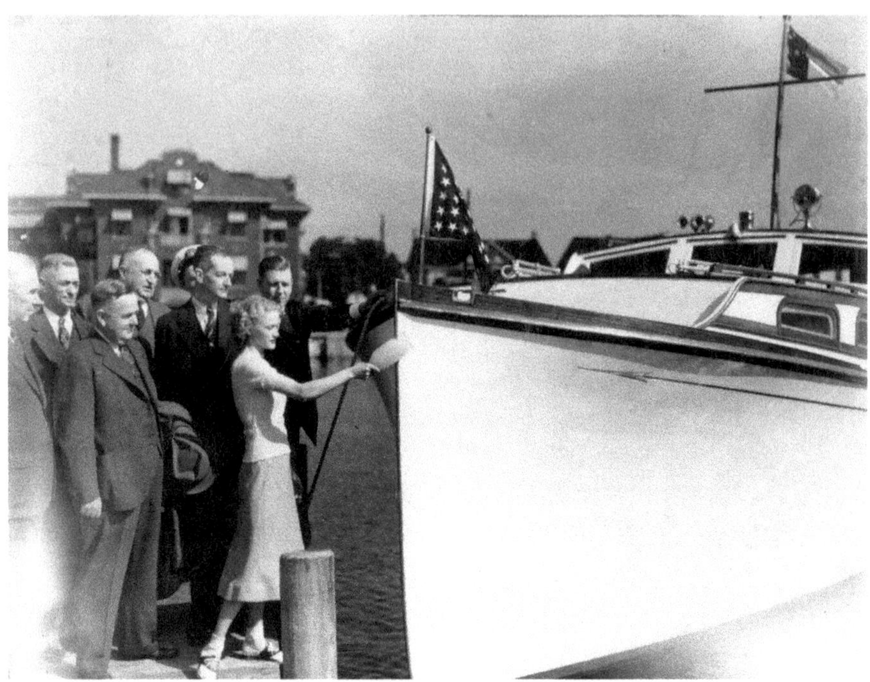

Catharine O'Bryan of Beaufort christens the state fisheries boat *Croatan* while members of the North Carolina Department of Conservation and Development look on. *North Carolina Department of Conservation and Development Photo Collection, State Archives of North Carolina, 1939.*

In addition to enforcing law, the Manteo-based *Croatan* was more or less a state-sponsored yacht/floating ambassador, ferrying bigwigs, eminentos and local and out-of-state press hounds who might share the virtues of the Carolina coast with their readers.

On *Croatan*'s shakedown cruise, Roanoke Island native R. Bruce Etheridge, director of the North Carolina Department of Conservation and Development, and commission members were joined by photographer Bill Baker of the State News Bureau, who snapped images that could be picked up by various newspapers and state promotional literature.

In 1941, *Croatan* and its sister ship, *Hatteras*, transported officials to Hatteras Island for a meeting with North Carolina governor J. Melville Broughton, who was touring the sandy outpost "for the purpose of inspecting roadways in that area and also a visit to all the lighthouses and coast guard stations in the area."

In 1952, when Governor W. Kerr Scott hosted Arkansas governor Sid McMath on a fishing trip out of Oregon Inlet with legendary captain Omie

Tillett, the press tried to keep tabs from a distance, cruising on the *Croatan* with Captain Basnight.

But Arnold J. "Ducky" Stewart probably put it best in his column Hunting and Fishing for Delaware's *Wilmington Morning News*, declaring, "When the Conservation Department of the State of North Carolina entertains a guest, 'he is well entertained.'"

Following a complimentary showing of *The Lost Colony* outdoor drama in August 1941, Stewart and Tom Basnight went fishing, bringing in an impressive catch of fourteen dolphin, sixteen bonito and twenty-one blues. "With fingers and arms aching it has been two days of swell outside salt-water fishing as a guest of a swell state." This is the kind of early publicity that roused outsiders to visit the Outer Banks for some offshore adventure.

Croatan kept watch over area waters for thirty-plus years, with an average cruising speed of twelve to sixteen knots, until its retirement in the early 1970s. But once Frank Turner purchased the surplus vessel from the state via sealed bid, he put it in a whole different state of dry-dock—while preserving the hospitality.

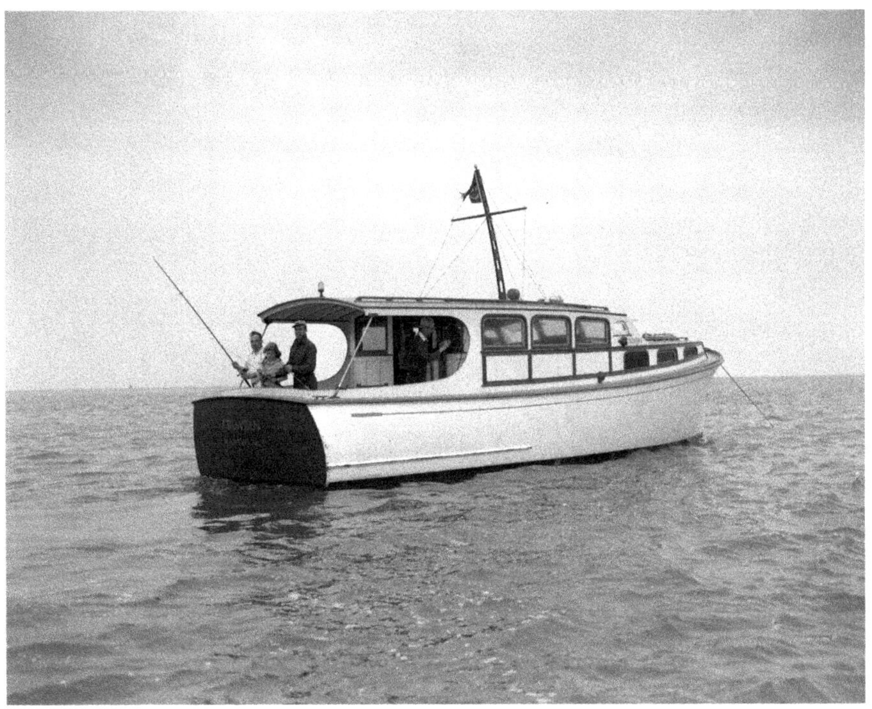

Fishing aboard the state fisheries boat *Croatan*. *North Carolina Department of Conservation and Development Photo Collection, State Archives of North Carolina, 1945.*

He started by hauling *Croatan* over to a Nags Head sand dune on the Beach Road near the Carefree Cottages—between mileposts fifteen and sixteen—upgrading it with "shoreside plumbing, and adding the kitchen and hot water heater." For $300 a week in season, a couple or a family of four with two small children could rent the *Croatan* as their summer vacation home.

Although it wasn't air-conditioned, Croatan featured "a head with spacious shower and a double bunk in the forward cabin. Two couches in the main salon convert to single beds." The old bridge (the platform from which the vessel was captained) was converted into a galley (boat-talk for kitchen). Accoutrements included "a mini-microwave, toaster oven, fridge, sink and television."

It served as a hospitable host for a number of years, but sometime in the mid-90s, the old girl slipped off the radar, most likely meeting its demise in a practice burn by the Nags Head Fire Department. While Fire Chief Kevin Zorc was unable to locate any specific paperwork, he checked with Pete Grana, Nags Head's first paid firefighter, who remembers burning it for training, but remains "fuzzy as to the exact date or essential details."

"Funny," Zorc said recently, "I can see the boat in my memory, and remember feeling sad that it was gone. Guess I viewed it as a cool alternative place to live; a victim of redevelopment."

Add another legendary ghost ship to the Outer Banks annals.

ONE BIG FISH, TWO BIG RECORDS

Jack Herrington and the "Grander"

Some records are meant to be broken, while others stand the test of time. On July 26, 1974, Jack Herrington hooked both world and state records when he landed the first Atlantic blue marlin weighing over 1,000 pounds. His 1,142-pound catch remained a world record for nearly three years, while the state record stood for over a quarter century. But landing the first "grander," now that's a heavy fish tale.

Herrington, of Allison Park, Pennsylvania, chartered *Jo Boy* out of Oregon Inlet, captained by Harry Baum. "It had been a good dolphin year," Herrington recalled, "and I told Harry that we'd love to catch some dolphin." In the Gulf Stream, they found the long lines of sargassum weed under which the dolphin, otherwise known as mahi-mahi, swim. Dozens of the brightly colored delicious game fish were landed. Then the party began to troll for marlin. The big fish hit around 10:30 a.m., "and it was a very interesting 2 hours and 45 minutes from that point on," mused Herrington, when interviewed by the author in 2007.

Captain Baum noticed the marlin "was pushing up the sea a foot high in front of him, like a porpoise." Finally, after thirty or forty-five minutes it finally jumped, but only two-thirds of its body came out of the water. "A two or three hundred-pound fish will jump 4, 5, 6, 7, 8 times. This fish never did that."

The marlin made several runs, taking out line before being reeled back in, only to then take more line out. Herrington had donned gloves and was thankful that the fighting chair on *Jo Boy* had a footrest. Mate Richard Baum,

Harry's nephew, brought out a brand-new harness that Herrington put on to ease the strain of the fight, but the contraption that was supposed to relieve his discomfort in fact created more. It had inadvertently been put on upside down and was burrowing into his side.

But Captain Baum kept Herrington's spirits up. "Don't you rest," Baum told him as Herrington continued to fight the fish. The marlin finally came to the surface on its side, worn out from the long fight. Baum had been on the radio to boats nearby, and with the help of one of them, they managed to slide the monster on board around 2:00 p.m.

On the way back to the fishing center, Herrington began to estimate the weight of his catch. "There was speculation that the fish might weigh more than 1,000 pounds. I weighed 160 pounds at that time and I watched that fish, and in my mind started to cut him up into 160-pound portions."

Via radio, news of the mammoth catch began to spread through the fleet and then onshore, and people began to assemble to await the arrival of *Jo Boy* and the marlin. Herrington's wife, Phoebe, and his three daughters were waiting at the docks. They had heard a large fish had been boated but didn't know who caught it. The angler could read his wife's lips silently asking, "Who? Who?" to which he silently mouthed, "Me! Me!"

With great care, the marlin was unloaded off the boat with the help of at least half a dozen mates and fish cleaners, but weighing the billfish proved difficult. The scales at Oregon Inlet Fishing Center didn't have enough counter weights for a catch that heavy, so the blue marlin was loaded into the back of a pickup truck and driven to the Hatteras Marlin Club, where it tipped the scales at 1,142 pounds, which surpassed the previous record by exactly 300 pounds. The thirteen-foot, ten-inch billfish attracted much attention from both the sportfishing and scientific communities as well as outdoor sports writers.

Herrington's world record fell in 1977, when a 1,282-pound blue marlin was caught off St. Thomas. Paulo Amorin holds the current world record, a 1,402-pounder that was landed in 1992 off Vitória, Brazil. In 2008, Trey Irvine of Fort Lauderdale, Florida, broke the North Carolina record when he boated a 1,228-pound fish while competing in the annual Pirate's Cove Billfish Tournament.

When asked how he felt when his record was broken, Herrington responded candidly, "Not badly at all. I always had conversations with myself and I knew records were meant to be broken. I put myself in the same category with the guy who first ran the four-minute mile or the guy who first climbed that mountain in the Himalayas; I was the first to catch an Atlantic blue marlin over 1,000 pounds."

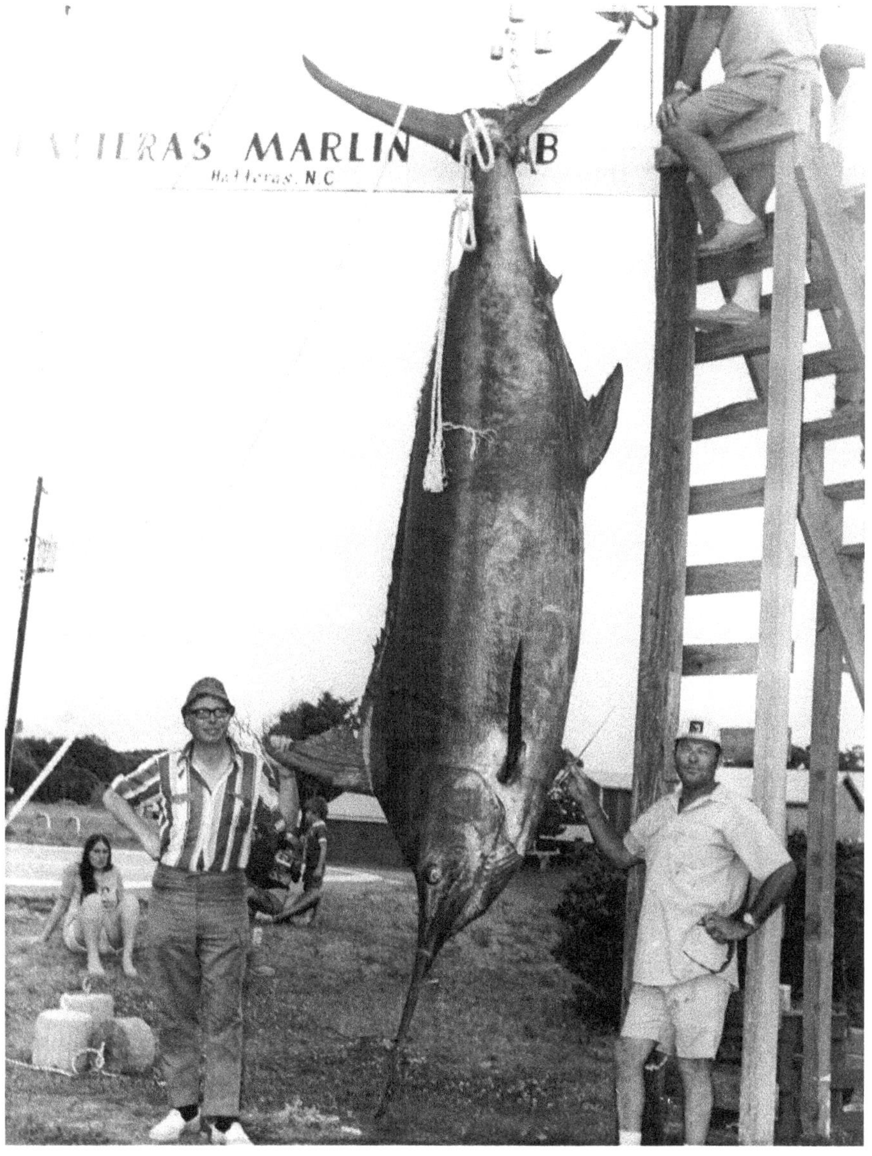

Jack Herrington *(left)* and Captain Harry Baum *(right)* pose with Herrington's world record 1,142-pound Atlantic blue marlin. *Aycock Brown Collection, Outer Banks History Center, 1974.*

Although larger fish have been landed, a mold of Jack Herrington's grander—the first Atlantic blue marlin taken weighing over one thousand pounds—can be seen in the display case at the Oregon Inlet Fishing Center.

NO MORE COURTEOUS A CAPTAIN

Martin Johnson and His Steamer Trenton *Were an Area Institution*

In the days before bridges and automobiles, travel to and from the Outer Banks was by boat. Sailing vessels and steam-powered ships brought vacationers for the day, the weekend, the week or in some cases the entire summer! One of the most well-known and beloved captains at the start of the twentieth century was Martin Johnson, "a tall, raw-boned Roanoke Islander," who was captain of the legendary *Hattie Creef*, the fishing sloop cum steamboat that made the rounds between Elizabeth City and Manteo between the waning days of the nineteenth century and 1914. Johnson was also a keen businessman who used his popularity and position in the community to monopolize boat travel on the waterways in the Albemarle region.

George Washington Creef Jr. built the *Hattie Creef*, which he named for his infant daughter. When *Hattie Creef* first launched in 1889, Creef used it as a fishing boat, but by the turn of the century, it was ferrying passengers and freight with regular service between Manteo and Elizabeth City, with stops at Nags Head both coming and going. The *Hattie Creef* left the dock at 5:00 a.m. and departed Elizabeth City at 1:30 p.m. for the return trip to Roanoke Island.

But along about 1914, the *Hattie Creef* was retired from this route, and a new steamer, *Guide*, replaced it. Captain Johnson also retired from the East Carolina Transportation Company and purchased his own vessel, the 165-foot *Trenton*, which was a great improvement to water travel in the Albemarle, as it was much faster and more comfortable than its

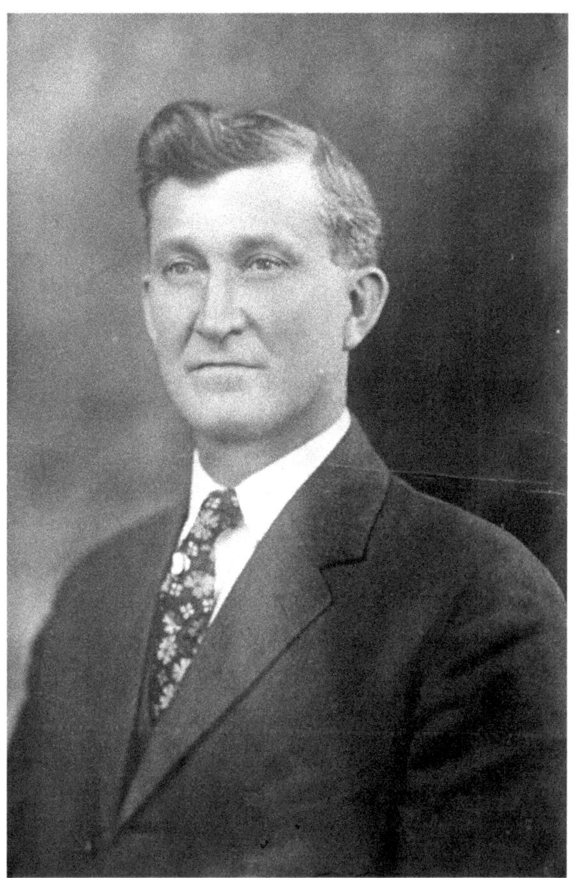

Captain Martin Johnson's career spanned over twenty-five years; consequently, he was one of the most well-known people in the Albemarle region. *Photo courtesy Linda Lau, circa 1930.*

predecessors and could make the trip from Elizabeth City to the Outer Banks in three and a half hours.

Johnson formed a partnership with Dr. Scott and "other prominent business men," operating what they called the Johnson Line, in direct competition with the East Carolina Transportation Company, Johnson's old employer. *Trenton* made its first trip between the Banks and Elizabeth City on July 13, 1914. What happened next could only be described as good old American entrepreneurial chutzpah.

One of the first changes Captain Johnson initiated after he began his routes on the *Trenton* was to cut his fare from one dollar to seventy-five cents, to which the East Carolina Transportation Company responded by cutting its fare in half, to fifty cents. Newspapers predicted that the rate war would be a boon to travelers because "both sides are determined to fight to the bitter end." And soon passengers would be paying a nickel.

However, within six weeks, Johnson and Scott bought out the East Carolina Transportation Company and merged the two lines.

Soon, Johnson was carrying the mail each day, as well as freight commodities, to Roanoke Island. By 1926, the East Carolina Transportation Company could brag of its longevity and staying power, "Sailing more than a million Miles, Carrying a Quarter Million Passengers," and Johnson's tenure was reaching legendary status. "On no other line in eastern North Carolina has the same master served as long as Capt. Martin Johnson. On no other line has a steamboat Captain sailed as far. Figure it up, 90 miles a day, six trips a week, and he has sailed over a million miles, equal to 350 trips across the Atlantic Ocean, or forty times around the world."

Six years later, Captain Johnson was featured in a special edition of the *Daily Advance* published on the occasion of the dedication of the Wright Brothers National Memorial, which again gives testament to the high esteem in which he was held:

> *No more courteous a captain ever stepped on the bridge of any vessel than Captain Martin Johnson. He is known to more people over the entire country than any other individual in Dare County, a statement that will stand up with out contradiction. His service to Dare County is inestimable in its value, for he is rated as one of the pioneers of building and development throughout the entire county.*

In order to keep up with the times, the *Trenton* underwent substantial renovations in 1927 and was fitted with a crude oil engine, which increased its speed and opened up additional cargo space, including enough room to offer a ferry service for personal vehicles. As many as eight cars could ride on her main deck.

But the days of water transportation and the era of Captain Martin Johnson would come to a close with changing times. By 1930, visitors to the Outer Banks were arriving in automobiles and buses via the new Wright Memorial Bridge and driving to their destinations along the Beach Road. Goods were trucked to the resort communities. Johnson had to cut the *Trenton*'s daily stop to Nags Head in order to save money.

In 1932, people of the Albemarle region were much dismayed when Captain Johnson lost the contract to deliver the mail to Manteo, where it was sent to the smaller waterfront hamlets in lighter vessels. The Virginia Dare Bus Line could deliver letters and packages faster and for less.

Without the money from the mail contract, Johnson could hardly afford to run the *Trenton.*

Another unfortunate event at the end of the Captain Johnson's career was the collision of the *Trenton* with the luxury yacht *Betsy L II* near Elizabeth City in May 1935. The private yacht was en route to New York from Florida when it was struck by the larger *Trenton.* It was the first accident in Johnson's thirty-year history on the *Trenton.* Alf Thompson, master of *Betsy L II,* filed a petition in Eastern District Court in Elizabeth City. Both sides claimed the other was at fault in the mishap, which took place when both vessels were trying to pass through the open drawbridge over the Pasquotank River. However, a private agreement was reached, and the charge was dismissed in 1936. That same year, W.S. Furnace of Norfolk purchased the *Trenton.* Captain Johnson retired and spent his remaining years living on Roanoke Island. He died in 1959 and is buried in Mount Olivet Cemetery.

ONE FISH, THREE FISH, SAWFISH, THIEVED FISH

It was typical morning in Nags Head in 1914. Men worked their nets in the great Atlantic, while summer people from the Unpainted Aristocracy—the original cottages built in the vicinity of Jockey's Ridge—spent the morning near the shore. Some strolled along the sand, while others swam before breakfast. Francis Winslow, a young attorney from Rocky Mount, North Carolina, whose family owned one of the archetypal Nags Head cottages, walked along the beach with his father, Frith. The pair came upon John Culpepper, a local fisherman, whom their summer neighbor James E. Wood recollected "kept the cottagers supplied with fish right out of the ocean for a 9 o'clock breakfast every morning." But this morning, Culpepper's net had been cut to pieces and he struck a deal with the Winslows.

Culpepper made an unfortunate haul that included a sawfish (*Pristis pectinatus*), a denizen of the sea distinguished by its bill or sword. Often three or four feet long, the sword is edged on either side with a row of twenty-four to thirty sharp teeth that gives the fish its name as well as its ability to shred a seine.

Sawfish, on occasion, are taken along the coast of North Carolina. For example, in 1949, Jimmy Swindell was shrimping in his trawler *Mary Josephine* when he netted an eight-hundred-pound sawfish at Beaufort Inlet, which attracted much attention when it was brought to the dock in Morehead City. During the summer of 1951, Captain Joe Jennette netted a fifteen-foot monster near the Cape Hatteras Lighthouse while fishing for bluefish. The beast was estimated to weigh over one thousand pounds.

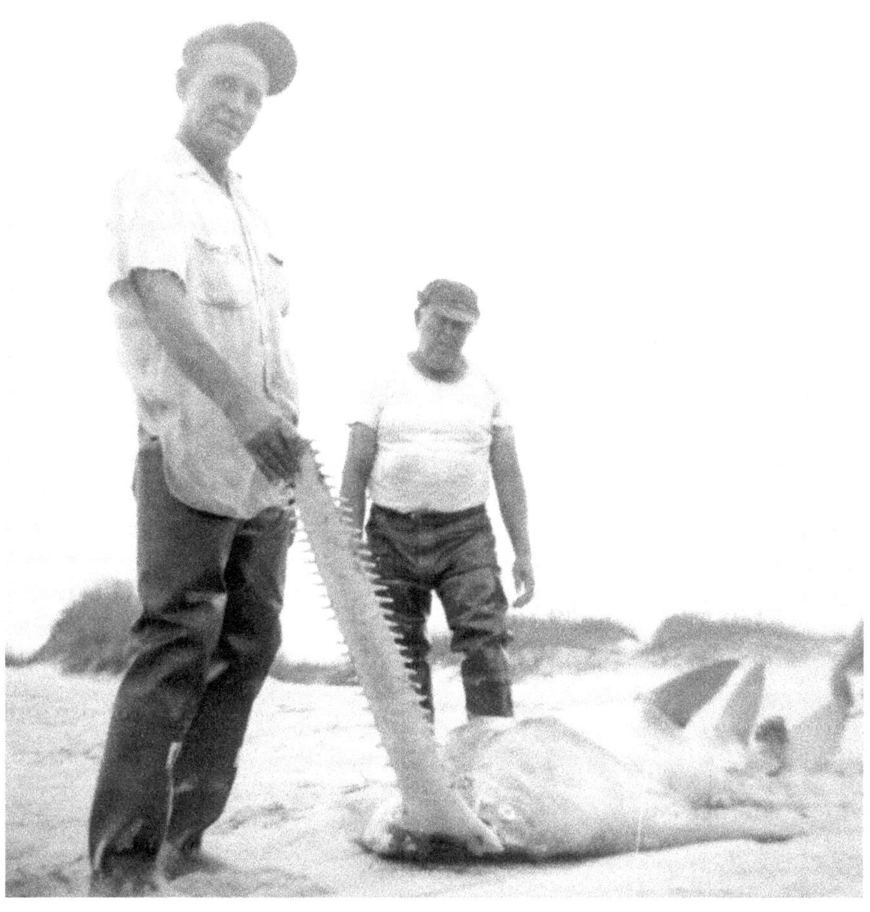

This eight-hundred-pound sawfish landed at Cape Hatteras is most likely the same fish described in newspaper accounts as the one netted by Joe Jennette. *Herbert Hutchinson Brimley Photograph Collection. Audio Visual Materials. State Archives of North Carolina, 1951.*

But on that Nags Head morning in 1914, John Culpepper removed the five-and-a-half-foot bill from the sawfish in his net and for one dollar and fifty cents sold it to the elder Winslow, who took his prize back to the cottage, where it was dried and then hung on display as a nautical curiosity. Around 1931, Francis Winslow, the successful Rocky Mount, North Carolina lawyer approaching middle age, took the childhood souvenir from his father's cottage and gave it a special place in his own new beach house—a one-and-a-half-story oceanfront cottage built by Stephen J. Twine. There the sawfish bill remained until the spring of 1969.

Sometime between April 6 and May 10, the sawfish bill was abducted. "Every guest in my house has commented on its removal and expressed indignation," Francis Winslow wrote in a letter to Nags Head police chief Donny Twyne. "I would very much like to recover this prized memento of John Culpepper's feat." The barrister also sent a signed copy of the same letter to the *Coastland Times* newspaper, which, on August 1, ran an article under the headline "Sawfish Bill Relic of the Deep Still Missing" that included excerpts from the letter and details surrounding the salacious sawfish bill swiping.

Cecelia Winslow was eight or nine years old when her grandfather's keepsake went missing. "It meant a lot to him," she recollected. "I'm sure whoever did it, did it as a prank."

Cecelia grew up coming to her family's cottage, and she too remembers the days watching fishermen work their nets in the surf. By then, John Culpepper had passed away, but Jethro Midgett still hauled seines on the beach.

Two weeks after portions of Francis Winslow's letter were printed in the *Coastland Times*, he penned another communiqué, this time a letter to the editor telling of the strange reappearance of the sawfish bill. It was discovered in the garage of a cottage two or three doors to the north. "It was returned to the Battle House. Kemp Battle was my granddaddy's law partner," explained Cecelia Winslow.

In fact, Battle and Winslow had been close friends and colleagues for nearly sixty years. At the University of North Carolina, both shared a penchant for debate and formed, along with friends Frank Porter Graham (also of Nags Head summer stock) and Charles W. Tillet Jr., a group known as the Pin Point Discussion Club. In 1911, they began practicing law together after founding the Battle and Winslow law firm.

"Our close relationship was well known to everyone who knew us, I do not know why it was returned to his house rather than mine, but I am sure that the person who returned it knew it would be returned to me."

And so, according to Cecelia Winslow, the bill was returned to its place on the cottage wall, which had faded over time and had a dark mark from where the relic hung. The Winslows knew it was the original because one of the teeth was broken and the imprint matched up exactly with the bill found in the Battles' garage. "I have no idea who took it, but I'm glad they returned it," she confessed.

FLOUNDER BEFORE FRIENDS

The day had been long anticipated. The autumn day when we would catch doormats—not just fourteen- or fifteen-inch flounder—but fish just a bit more substantial. Fish just a bit thicker. When I crossed over the dune at Oregon Inlet that Sunday morning with the sun and breeze in my face, and when I saw the crystal-clear green water, I knew my behavior the night before was justified. I had already been rewarded.

You see, all the weekend's fishing had to be squeezed in on Sunday, because of our friend Brian's wedding on Saturday. Our old fishing and football buddy was finally tying the knot. Sacrificing a prime fall fishing day for this once-in-a-lifetime event was legitimate, but nothing was going to keep me from Sunday's prime air and water temperatures, wind conditions and eager fish ready for nourishment with the onslaught of autumn.

Upon our return from the wedding reception, we found a note taped to our door and read it with dismay:

> *Hey now! We're down for the weekend! Came by but you weren't home. We're at Mike and Angie's. We'll be over soon.*
> *Love, Clemmie and Wynne*

"Oh no!" we bemoaned. It was the worst. Out-of-town visitors from Charlotte. Night owls. These folks had never seen a beach in the morning except by mistake when their late nights lasted until dawn. I quickly

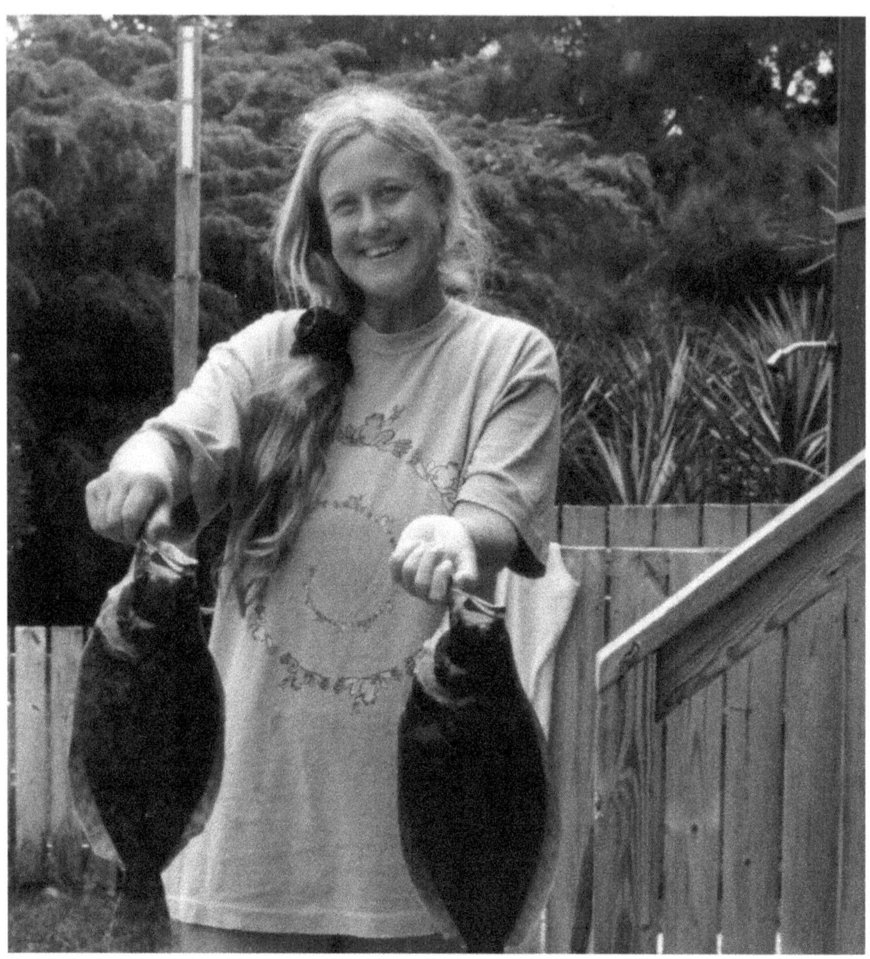

The author with a catch of Ocracoke flounder. *Collection of the author,* circa *1996.*

hardened. "Well they can come over," I quipped to my husband, "but they're not interfering with my fishing."

When our guests arrived at dusk, I was gracious and friendly. "It's barely 9:00," I thought. "I can be in bed by midnight and up early tomorrow." As the hours passed, my champagne-filled afternoon began to take its toll. At 11:30, I tactfully excused myself, explaining that my full day and the lateness of the hour had worn me out. Certainly, my guests would keep it quiet, or better yet, maybe they would even leave!

But they were having too much fun. I waited until 1:00, that's when their fun was beginning to interfere with mine. That's when I became assertive.

"Coming back to join us?" asked Clemmie when she saw me return. The dimly lit smoke-filled living room, the hour and the atmosphere made me feel like a stranger in my own house, but it was just that, my house. The house of an avid fisherwoman!

"It's 1:00," I stated, sounding like my mother used to, breaking in on my slumber parties. "I'm going fishing tomorrow. I need to be asleep. You all are too loud. If you stay here, you must whisper. I'm going to sleep now."

Back to bed I went, wondering who was rude, me or my guests? Twenty minutes later, dear husband joined me after bidding farewell to our partyers and sending them out in the warm, damp autumn night. We giggled for a few minutes before drifting off to sleep, dreaming of short sharp tugs at the end of our fishing lines.

We can't remember if we caught any other fish the following morning, but the pair of seventeen-inch and solo nineteen-inch flounder will be remembered for the rest of our lives. The day itself was gorgeous, perfect for fall fishing. I could easily have missed the action by staying up late catching up with our unexpected company. But now I have my priorities straight. I now prefer flounder before friends.

PART III

INNOVATIVE IDEAS

MADE IN THE SHADE

How Mission 66 Architecture Helped Create Coquina Beach

In 2016, the National Park System celebrated its centennial. All across America, historic sites, seashores, battlefields and trails preserved by the federal government held special events. But a half century ago, the parks were just spiffing up for their fifty-year anniversary. You might say they were on a mission. Indeed they were: Mission 66.

It was National Park Service director Newton Drury who first sought funding to modernize and update facilities and improve access to parks. After years of neglect during World War II, these national treasures experienced a visitation boom. Folks were eager for recovery, and Drury knew updates were necessary for the convenience and safety of the traveling public. However, it was his successor, Conrad Wirth (you might've ridden a ferry named for him on your way to Ocracoke), who implemented the idea.

Instead of asking for annual appropriations, Wirth requested a ten-year chunk of money, allowing for greater flexibility to accomplish multi-year projects. In 1956, they launched Mission 66 to fund maintenance and repair, construction of roads and trails and build visitor centers that would mark a new era. According to Dr. Sarah Allaback in her report *Mission 66 Visitor Centers: A History of a Building Type*, these new public facilities "were intended to blend into the landscape, but through their plainness rather than by identification with natural features." While prewar structures were rustic in nature, the new designs used "efficient and economical building materials, such as concrete, glass, and steel, which were thought less difficult to maintain and suited for high-traffic use."

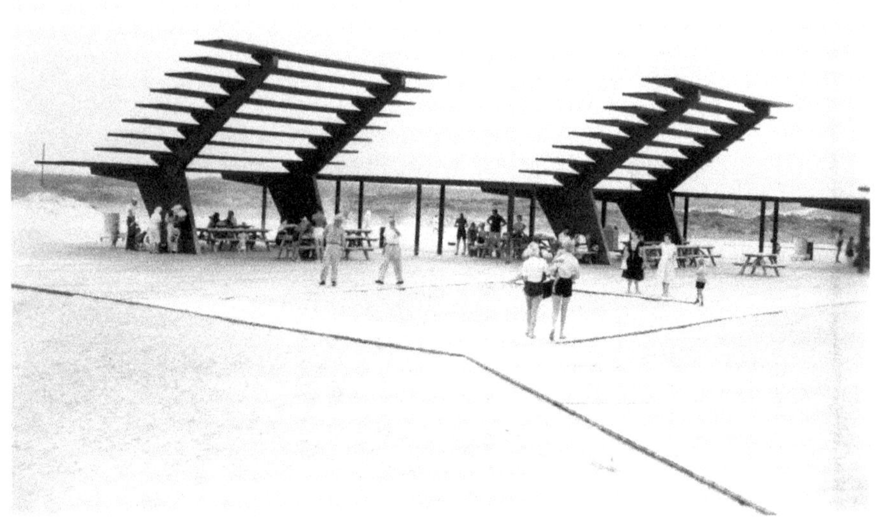

Award-winning futuristic sunshades at the Bodie Island Day Use Area were part of the National Park Service's Mission 66 initiative. *Courtesy of National Park Service, Cape Hatteras National Seashore, circa 1962.*

The Outer Banks soon became home to two modern-looking Mission 66 projects: the construction of the glass-domed visitor center at the Wright Brothers National Memorial, and the creation of a day-use area at Coquina Beach—part of the newly established Cape Hatteras National Seashore—including a set of sunshades made from cantilevered beams with horizontal louvers, rising like giant stairsteps.

But the sunshades at Coquina Beach Day Use Area weren't just futuristic-looking, they were meant to be functional. Designed by Donald Benson, an architect in the Park Service's Eastern Office of Design and Construction, the shades needed to shelter the picnic area but had to stand up to the Outer Banks' notorious storms and ever-moving sand, so they were built to allow hurricane winds to pass directly through them. (Originally, the beams were to be made of concrete and shades of metal, but plans were modified; Rilco Laminated Wood Products Company in St. Paul, Minnesota, made the prefabricated louvers from red cedar and fir and then sent them east for assemblage at Coquina Beach.)

Daniels Building Supply and Shanaberger Lumber Company of Nags Head received the $78,000 bid to put together the structures in the spring of 1956. They completed their task in October.

Locals and visitors were quick to take advantage of this new seaside gathering spot. One of the first documented uses of the picnic area was on October 13 when Balfour Baum Jr., whose father was a ranger at the Cape Hatteras National Seashore, celebrated his birthday at Coquina Beach with an "outdoor supper" complete with cake. Church picnics, family reunions and Girl Scout outings all partied in the shade. In June and July 1957, nearly thirty thousand people visited the Coquina Beach Day Use Area.

The shades also garnered national attention—both good and bad. While *Progressive Architecture* magazine highlighted the award-winning design, writer Dan Morrill felt that Benson's creation was possibly too forward-thinking, suggesting it might cause as much comment as "three nude men on a Republican Convention Program," until modern architecture became the norm.

Although designed for hurricane-force winds and encroaching sand, the eye-catching architecture proved no match for series of good old Outer

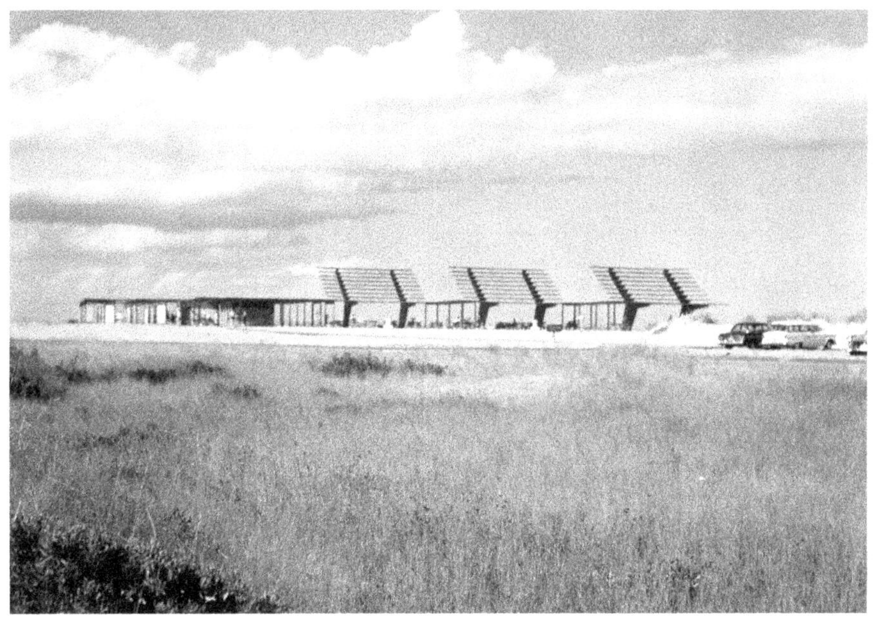

Improvements at the Bodie Island Day Use Area included paved parking, bathrooms, showers and covered picnic tables. *Courtesy of National Park Service, Cape Hatteras National Seashore, circa 1957.*

Banks nor'easters. In April 1973, the *Coastland Times* ran a photograph under the headline "Coquina Picnic Area Falls Prey to Sea." The caption explained the picnic area was "a victim of severe storms and erosion this past winter," and went on share the gloomy news that "the picnic platform and the sunshades shown here have been partially destroyed by encroaching water and will be torn down in the near future."

Still, many Mission 66 structures remain—including a sister site in KDH. In fact, the Wright Brothers National Memorial visitor center recently underwent renovations that returned the historic structure to its original form, updated the displays and made the building "greener."

Get out to our national parks and see them. It's a big country. You need a mission.

A BLAST FROM THE PAST

Corolla Rockets and the Race for Space

In 1961, a cosmonaut named Yuri Gagarin became the first human to orbit the earth. Suddenly, the United States found itself chasing Soviet technology at the height of the Cold War. A year later, President John F. Kennedy was asking Congress for $7–$9 billion to fund aeronautics research, challenging Americans to put a man on the moon by the end of the decade.

"No nation which expects to be the leader of other nations," he told a packed stadium at Rice University on September 12, 1962, "can expect to stay behind in the race for space." But for America's tech community, the race was already on. Bolstered by a $500,000 contract with the U.S. Air Force, the Virginia-based Atlantic Research Corporation was developing a pasty concoction called "gel-solid," which it believed would generate the necessary thrust to power rockets and become "the workhorse for outer space exploration." They just needed a place to test it.

In April 1961, North Carolina officials learned of Atlantic Research's quest and provided social and economic data, aerial photographs and tax information about Corolla—a sparsely populated area between the Virginia line and Duck. The company would ultimately lease a parcel of land owned by out-of-town title holders called the Whalehead Club, which included the 1925 art deco mansion and numerous outbuildings built as a hunting club for industrialist Edward Knight and his wife, Marie Louise. Also acquired for the rocket testing site were eight miles of oceanfront property and two abandoned Coast Guard buildings.

An announcement was made in April 1962 that North Carolina had "stepped into the space age." Newspaper articles foretold how the project would breathe new life into the secluded village and create jobs and prosperity. It was predicted that by the dawn of 1963, Atlantic Research Corporation would have between seventy-five and one hundred employees "working on two space age problems."

"Consider the time and place," says Susan Joy Davis, who delved deeply into each era of the great estate for her book *The Whalehead Club: Reflections of Currituck Heritage*. "They were pioneers in the development of advanced performance solid-fuels for ballistic missiles during an urgent and heightened national effort to excel beyond Soviet capabilities."

At the time, the relatively new company didn't have a mobile workforce to relocate to Corolla. Instead, it hoped to recruit "mechanically inclined young men"—sorry, ladies—from inside eastern North Carolina. In total, Atlantic Research Corporation employed eight people full-time; one commuted down the beach from Virginia; four rode over on a boat from Coinjock; and three were Corolla residents. Currituck native Travis Morris remembers the cautious nature of the site and the corporation's commitment to keep everyone else out.

"They wouldn't let you around the Club," the outgoing octogenarian recalled. "There were No Trespassing signs up and you couldn't even go into the boat basin. You couldn't drive around up there."

Perhaps it was for the best. Powdered beryllium used in the propellant mix was toxic, the explosives used to fire the rockets were dangerous and secret details of the experiment made safety and security a top priority. In fact, while the company hoped the state would one day connect the road between Duck and Corolla to support a larger facility—future plans included a rocket manufacturing plant with three hundred to four hundred workers—that would have altered the secluded nature of the Currituck Banks that was necessary for rocket testing.

The United States would end up winning the Space Race by putting a man on the moon in July 1969. Ironically, that same year, the Atlantic Research Corporation closed shop in Corolla, leaving behind several storage buildings and Quonset huts. Within a couple decades, the final piece of Route 12 would connect northern beaches to the mainland, launching a tourism boom that still echoes today—and eliminating all the memories of Corolla's early experiment with rocket science.

ICE IS NICE

The History of Chillin' on the Outer Banks

So, it's Saturday morning. You and your besties are headed out for an Outer Banks day trip. Maybe a surfing or fishing trek to Hatteras. Perhaps a picnic at Jockey's Ridge or Festival Park. That means packing a cooler with ice. Today, you might empty your freezer or swing by 7-Eleven, but two hundred years ago frozen water was no everyday convenience. It was a precious resource that traveled for hundreds of miles—arriving in half-ton blocks instead of ten-pound bags.

In their book *When Ice Came to the Outer Banks*, Alvah H. Ward Jr. and R. Wayne Gray describe how not even Thoreau's Walden Pond was safe from a fledgling ice industry as "schooners flying down the coast from Maine and Massachusetts [were] loaded with 500-pound chunks of ice that had been cut from the ponds and lakes of New England."

It stayed that way for nearly a century. Upon ice's arrival, Outer Banks fish houses stored the blocks in icehouses filled with sawdust as insulation. When it finally melted, fishermen did without. With no commercial ice plants on Roanoke Island, fish could spoil quickly and the seafood industry could grow no larger than supplying nearby ports like Elizabeth City. But once entrepreneurs began producing ice locally, it became the necessary catalyst to fuel a whole range of industries, from commercial and recreational fishing to tourism—even if it took a few tries to finally take hold.

During the late nineteenth century, a short-lived ice plant operated in the vicinity of Skyco, at that time Roanoke Island's busiest port. The next two facilities were built on Manteo's working waterfront. According to Ward and Gray, "The second ice plant in Dare County was built on the east side of Dough's creek" and used steam power to produce "probably a capacity of ten to fifteen tons." It burned after a quarter century of service, but its memory lingers in the name Ice Plant Island, now home to the *Elizabeth II* and Roanoke Island Festival Park.

Around 1923, the People's Ice and Storage Company became the county's third ice producer. It too melted away, one of the many buildings lost in the great fire of September 1939.

Ultimately, Alvah Ward Sr. would be the man to bring long-lasting, commercial ice production to Dare County. A Roanoke Island native, he returned home after a brief stint as a tanker engineer for the Standard Oil Company. He married Tracie Cahoon, a Wanchese gal, and traded in his years at sea and invested in his local community.

In 1929, Ward was given the opportunity to build an ice plant near the Globe Fish Company at a spot called Wanchese Wharf on Roanoke Island's lower west side. The location tapped into an artesian well of cool, clean water. It also allowed the fish company's vessels to transport ice "throughout Pamlico, Roanoke and Croatan Sounds—from Hatteras to Mashoes Landing." Meanwhile, trucks made daily deliveries to cottage owners and businesses that catered to the vacation trade.

In Susan Rountree's book *Nags Headers*, Carmen Gray shared stories about her uncle Jethro Midgett, who delivered ice to summer people and had quite a following among the young ladies.

"It would come over in 300 pound cakes and he would take his ice pick and block it off in a hundred pounds; a hundred pounds, and then fifty; fifty....He'd put it in this army truck he had...and take around the ice."

Numerous oral history interviews housed at the Outer Banks History Center are peppered with memories of women who waited for a glimpse of the tan, muscular Midgett as he made his rounds.

In 1947, Alvah Ward Sr. enlarged and modernized Dare County Ice and Storage and built a new brick building on the main drag through Manteo. (The building survives today as the Roanoke Island Outfitters and Dive Center.) But by the late 1940s, demand dwindled as commercial icemakers became available for numerous restaurants and hotels that defined the post–World War II tourism boom.

Alvah Ward Sr. died in 1952. His wife, Tracie, took over the business while longtime employee Bow Tillet ran the plant. When Alvah Jr. was able to return home from the military, Tillet taught him how to operate the facility.

After an admirable run filled with challenges such as coastal tempests, aging equipment and an exploding diesel engine that caused "an irate delegation of housewives…wanting redress for their laundry sprayed with oil"—not to mention a cold storage accident that took part of a finger—Alvah Ward Jr. sold Dare County Ice and Storage in 1973. The purchaser, Wood Beasley, later sold to Southern Ice, which built a larger facility in Kill Devil Hills. The company later sold to Reddy Ice, which today slings crystal cubes from commercial kitchens to convenience stores.

So, there you have it. The cold hard truth. Now pack that cooler and get to the beach.

HIGH PRAISE

From the First High-Rise Hotel to the First Liquor Drinks, Alice Sykes Pushed the Limits of Outer Banks Innovation

If the *Coastland Times*' front page for June 29 was any indication, the summer of 1951 was shaping up swell. *The Lost Colony* was set to run its eleventh season. The famed Nags Head Casino would host the Dixie Rhythm Boys. And the new Sea Ranch Hotel was ready to open just north of Kitty Hawk. Over the next fifty years, this "strikingly different" and "exclusive retreat" would grow into a major resort—and change the face of Outer Banks hospitality.

"This is when they were first developing Southern Shores and later Colington Island," said Clifford Blakely of Kill Devil Hills, who not only worked for Alice for thirty years, but also married her eldest grandchild, Margo Powell. "Alice and her contemporaries changed us from more of a local resort to beginning the rise of tourism on the Outer Banks. From there, it just grew."

The Sea Ranch was the brainchild of Mr. and Mrs. Travis Sykes, otherwise known as Buck and Alice. The couple was originally from Virginia Beach, where Alice got her start in the hospitality business. After spending winters in California, New Mexico and Florida, the Gates County, North Carolina native decided she wanted to bring a new style of hotel to the Outer Banks. One that would capture the people's imaginations and draw tourists from places besides nearby Elizabeth City and Virginia's Tidewater region.

The "California-styled Sea Ranch with every room facing the ocean" was part of the building boom following World War II. Nags Head's Carolinian Hotel set the standard of modern hostelry on the Outer Banks when it began receiving guests in 1947, but the Sea Ranch garnered its fair share of visitors and special events. (The hotel's early guests included a group of seven first ladies of North Carolina and the Irish ambassador to the United States.) But it was her knack for selling fresh ideas to new markets that set Alice apart.

In 1954, Pirate's Week featured a "buccaneer's banquet, treasure hunts, a pirate's costume ball, plank walking and other merriment." (Perhaps serving as inspiration for the county-wide Dare Beaches Pirate's Jamboree that drew crowds between 1955 and 1964?) But even more savvy was a 1959 weeklong event encouraging older visitors to bring their grandchildren to the Sea Ranch.

The S.O.G.W.P.I.P. Week (that's Silly Old Grandparents with Picture in Pocket in case you didn't recognize the acronym) used the slogan "Bring the Real Thing and Leave the Pictures Behind." Kiddies could swim, hike or even get a ride on the resident burro, Tequila. Meanwhile, attendants stood by to supervise the young folk so the adults might have a minute for their own entertainment.

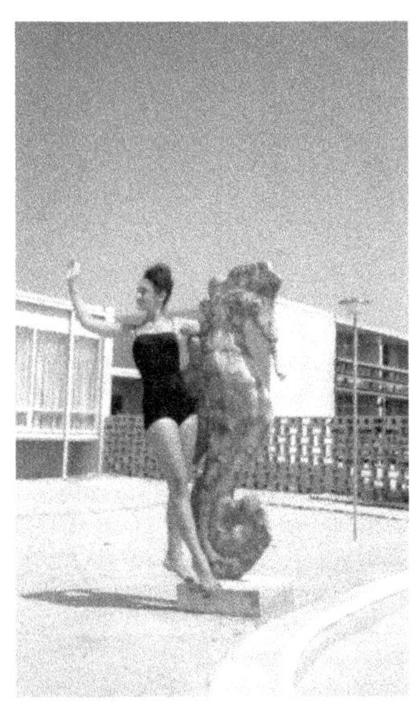

The "California-Style" Sea Ranch in Southern Shores featured rooms facing the ocean and a swimming pool. The seahorse has been its symbol for many years. *Aycock Brown Collection, Outer Banks History Center, circa 1951.*

Things stayed sunny at the Sea Ranch for the first full decade—until the winter of '62 when the Ash Wednesday Storm caused irreparable damage to the hotel. Rather than shut down, Alice took the setback as an opportunity. The following year, she opened a new twenty-six-room Sea Ranch at its new oceanfront location in Kill Devil Hills. And on December 29, 1967, Alice raised the bar again—along with building height—when the Sea Ranch broke ground on what would become first "high-rise" along the Outer Banks: "five stories of steel, charcoal brick and pink mortar."

Not to worry. The addition included an elevator—purported to be the first on Dare County's beaches. Later, the Sea Ranch would open the Outer Banks' first indoor pool (1973) and first indoor tennis facility (1979).

Over the years, more hotels came along, but Alice never ceased looking for ways to stand apart. She once traveled to Paris with dining room and lounge manager Patti Livengood in hopes of importing some traditional French cuisine to Kill Devil Hills. And she was just as active making moves in the community at large, including playing a role in bringing liquor-by-the-drink to certain townships in Dare County in 1980. One ABC official claims that Alice was first in line in Raleigh to procure a liquor license for the Sea Ranch and then to load up on liquor at the Nags Head ABC store—a rumor that Blakely recollects is only half-true.

"Holiday Inn got the first license," mused the longtime manager. "But the Sea Ranch sold the first mixed drink."

And that's high praise for the hard-partying Outer Banks.

But at its heart, the Sea Ranch was always a family business. (Blakely bought the Sea Ranch from Alice in 1990.) In 2012, it sold to partners—seven years after Alice Sykes passed away at the age of ninety-seven. But even with different owners, the Sea Ranch remains a lasting monument to one of our beach's boldest pioneers.

"She wasn't always right but she did things her way," Blakely candidly recalled. "And when she got her mind set on something, it was done."

FATHER OF THE FLEXIBLE WING

Francis Rogallo

The windswept Outer Banks are home to hundreds of retirees who move to the area after distinguished careers in a variety of vocations. The local community and the field of aviation lost a special member in September 2009 with the passing of Francis Melvin Rogallo, the inventor of the flexible wing.

Rogallo was born in Sanger, California, in 1912. After earning a degree in mechanical engineering and aeronautics at Stanford University, he took a position in Hampton, Virginia, with the National Advisory Committee for Aeronautics (the predecessor of NASA) in 1936. He met and married Hampton native Gertrude Sugden (1914–2008) in 1939.

The couple dreamed of creating a method of making simple inexpensive flight accessible for sport and recreation. Together, they worked to create the flexible wing (aka the Rogallo wing) in 1948. In fact, the first successful prototype was created from some of Gertrude's old curtains. They patented their invention and began to market the Flexi-Kite, which, due to its lack of rigidity, was able to perform stunts.

Shortly after the kite's debut in 1953, Rogallo described it in a United Press International article that ran in newspapers across the country. "It is flexible, non-rigid. There are no stays or braces of any rigid material. It consists of a square piece of plastic cloth folded down the middle. It has shroud lines like a parachute. It has the conventional lead string and tail. In flight, it appears to flap its wings like a bird."

Rogallo's brother Vernon, also a brilliant aeronautical engineer, demonstrated and marketed the Mylar Flexi-Kite on the West Coast, where he worked for NASA's Ames Research Center. Vernon and family, garbed in matching outfits his wife, June, made from red parachute material, performed as The Rockets, wowing West Coast audiences with demonstrations of the Flexi-Kite in the San Francisco Bay area.

In 1962, the Rogallos gave their patent to the United States government, to advance the country's technological capabilities in the rapidly emerging space program. Testing began almost immediately. NASA's Space Task Group hoped that the new technology could be used to land space capsules in the Gemini Program. Trials were done at Langley, and a new contraption, the Paresev (short for Paraglider Research Vehicle) was assembled and experimented at NASA's Dryden Center in Edwards, California. However, after much testing and great expense, parachutes were selected as the method for Gemini landings, but the information gleaned was not for naught.

The invention of the flexible wing was the springboard for many sports enjoyed today on the Outer Banks, and especially at Jockey's Ridge State

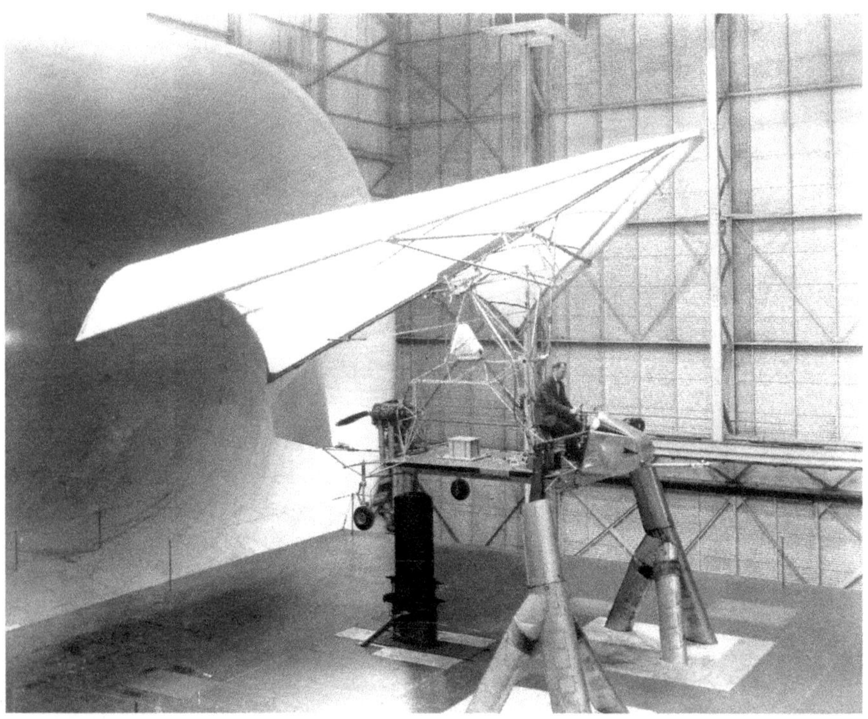

Testing the Rogallo parawing in a full-scale wind tunnel at the Langley Research Center in Hampton, Virginia. *NASA photo 62-631, 1962.*

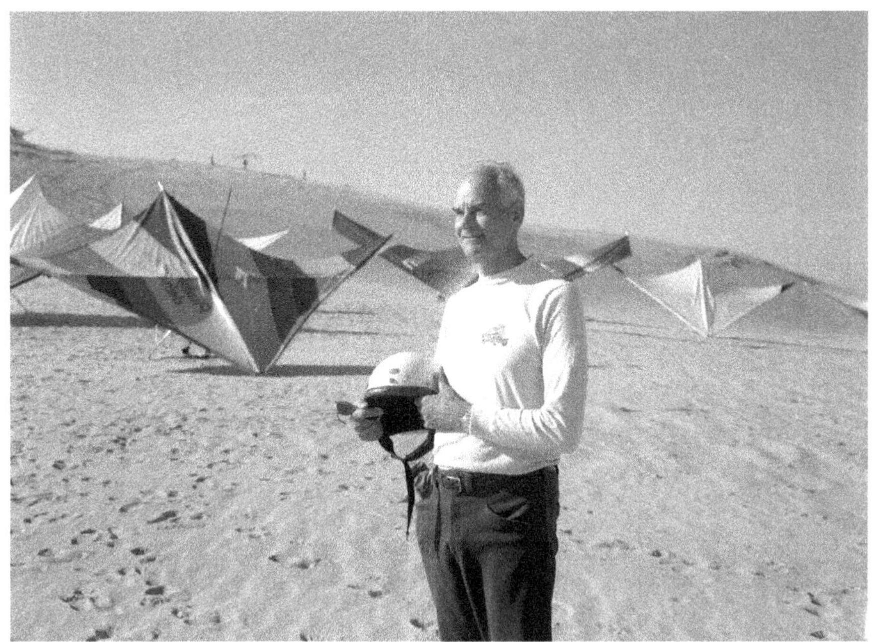

Francis Rogallo at Jockey's Ridge. *From the Hugh Morton Photographs and Films #P0081, copyright late 1970s or early 1980s, North Carolina Collection, University of North Carolina at Chapel Hill Library.*

Park—hang gliding, kiting and kiteboarding, which is ever increasing in popularity. According to Bruce Weaver, hang gliding manager at Kitty Hawk Kites in Nags Head, "It was the Rogallo wing that started it all. That invention led to the development of hang gliders, paragliders, ultralights, sport parachutes, delta kites, stunts kites, parafoil kites and kiteboarding kites. I don't know of many people who have been responsible for bringing so much joy to so many people. His invention has allowed millions of people to experience the magic of flight, either through flying themselves or by flying kites."

In 1967, Francis and Gertrude Rogallo purchased a vacation home in the development of Southern Shores and eventually retired to the Outer Banks community, where they were often seen at aviation events and hang-gliding and kiting contests and fly-ins. "Back in the '70s, Mr. Rogallo flew his hang glider regularly out on Jockey's Ridge," Weaver said. "Although he took his last flight on his eightieth birthday, Mr. Rogallo would still come out on the dune to see and talk to people flying their kites and gliders."

Francis Rogallo, or "Rog" as he was known, was inducted to the North Carolina Sports Hall of Fame in 1987. Eight years later, the Rogallos were honored internationally for their achievements in aviation. In 1995, they were inducted into the First Flight Shrine at the Wright Brothers National Memorial, where their likeness hangs in the portrait gallery. Francis was awarded the National Air and Space Museum Trophy in 1992 for his lifetime achievements in aviation. The Rogallo Kite Festival is held at Jockey's Ridge each June.

The Outer Banks attract all types: lovers, dreamers, artists, writers and even scientists. We are blessed to have walked the same sands as Francis Rogallo, a man who truly changed the world.

PART IV

CHANGING LANDSCAPES

A TOWN FIT FOR A QUEEN

Manteo's Mid-80s Makeover Was Meant for Royalty—but Remains Today

Roanoke Island loves to celebrate its status as birthplace of a nation. Over the years, the Outer Banks has gotten a lot of mileage out of the story of Sir Walter Raleigh's Roanoke voyages and the ill-fated colonists' failed attempt at a permanent English foothold in America between 1584 and 1587. In 1921, Dare County superintendent of schools Mabel Evans convinced the North Carolina Department of Public Instruction to fund a silent movie about the colonists, and of course, Paul Green penned *The Lost Colony* in 1937 as something of a 350-year salute. So, when the 400th anniversary of the Roanoke Voyages approached, not only Roanoke Islanders, but people across North Carolina prepared for a major party.

Although Her Majesty Queen Elizabeth II was invited to the festivities, it was her daughter, Her Royal Highness Princess Anne, who attended the dedication of the representative sixteenth-century sailing ship *Elizabeth II* on the first day of the opening celebration. Earlier that morning, officials named the bridge connecting Manteo with Ice Plant Island—known today as Roanoke Island Festival Park—the Cora Mae Daniels Basnight Bridge in honor of the Manteo native who played the role of Agona in *The Lost Colony* for a quarter century. During the afternoon, the princess and five hundred invited guests enjoyed a private luncheon at Elizabethan Gardens. It was said that the ham biscuits were of particular interest to the English guests as they were a "delicacy" that was "new to them."

The following day, a seventy-five-boat flotilla sailed from Elizabeth City with legendary newsman Walter Cronkite leading the procession. He came

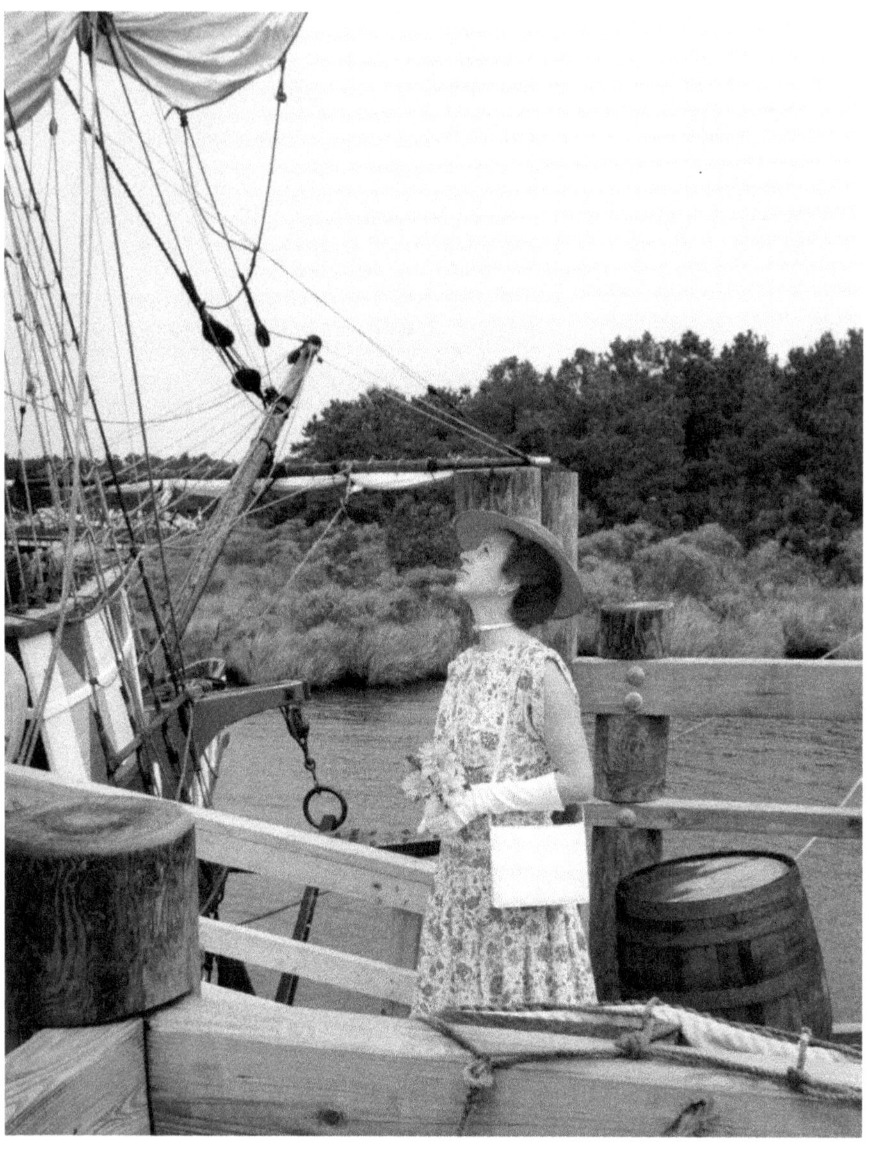

Her Royal Highness Princess Anne, daughter of Queen Elizabeth, attended the dedication of the *Elizabeth II,* the representative sixteenth-century sailing ship berthed in Manteo. *Joe Ernst Collection, Outer Banks History Center, 1984.*

ashore in Manteo and presented a 400th-anniversary banner to commissioner Harry Schiffman. The CBS anchorman received a few gifts in return, including an honorary membership in the Roanoke Island Yacht Club and a lifetime membership in the Friends of *Elizabeth II.* In the evening, the North Carolina Symphony played to an appreciative audience, and a fireworks display ended the night.

It was big—*really big*—but the revelry was more than a historic rager. Several lasting changes to the landscape transpired that are still enjoyed by residents and guests. The idea of America's 400th anniversary set many projects in motion that shaped the late-twentieth-century Outer Banks. "The likes of which the area had not seen," said local photographer and gallery owner Eve Trow Turek.

In the early '80s, Turek was a reporter with the *Outer Banks Current* newspaper. Covering town and county meetings was part of her "beat" back when plans were put in place to ensure that when the world's eyes were on Manteo and Roanoke Island, the town and the island looked good. She would eventually land a position as a county liaison to the state committee, a role that evolved into the Dare County public information officer.

Living in a downtown Manteo apartment during that time, "I woke up every day to the sound of hammers," she said of the construction of the *Elizabeth II,* "and was able to see progress on the ship each day." The idea of having a vessel moored across from the Manteo waterfront was "to have something tangible to help tell the story of the colonists."

Eve credits architect and conservationist John F. Wilson IV for many of the transformations that took place. Wilson, a Roanoke Island native, ran for mayor of Manteo in order to help steer the direction of the celebration and subsequent outcomes. "John had…such a caring and vision for his hometown. He was adamant that the town's people were involved with how the town grew, planned and developed."

Consultants from the North Carolina State University School of Design were brought in to "sit on front porches" with town residents and to "pick their brains and pluck their hearts." Manteo would receive national and international attention and "wanted to be ready to play host" for the 400th.

Roads and infrastructure received upgrades, billboards got kicked to the curb, landscaping projects bloomed and one thousand trees took root. Even the new route selected to funnel visitors directly into Manteo got a new name: Highway 400. The waterfront shops and the expansion of the public docks all remain part of the legacy.

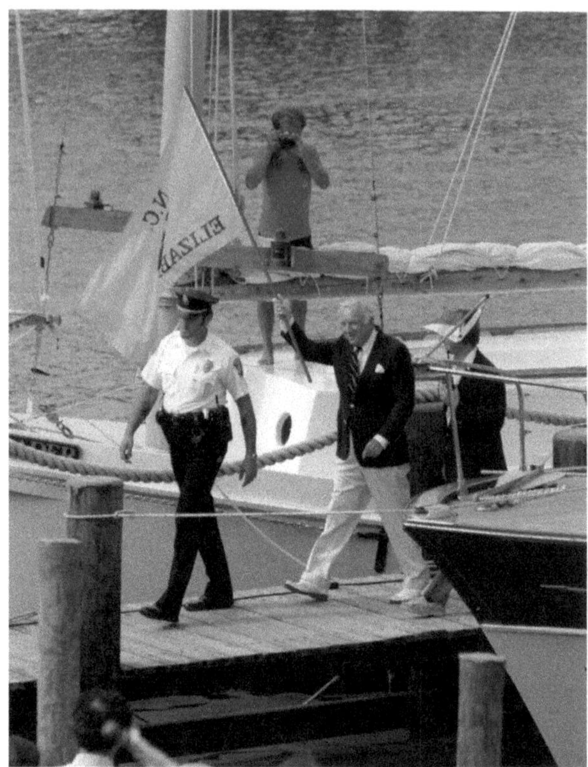

Walter Cronkite comes ashore at Manteo after leading a seventy-five-vessel flotilla from Elizabeth City. *Joe Ernst Collection, Outer Bank History Center, 1984.*

Angel Khoury gives a succinct summation in her 1999 book, *Manteo: A Roanoke Island Town*. The author suggests that the rundown Manteo waterfront in the early 1980s "was a far cry from being a fitting place to entertain the Queen of England," which motivated Wilson and the Manteo Board of Commissioners "not just to see Manteo become the site of a short-lived celebration—but to achieve a much more far-reaching goal—the economic and aesthetic revitalization of the Town of Manteo."

So, while Roanoke Island spruced itself up to receive Princess Anne, it was the rest of us who really got the real royal treatment.

YOU ARE HERE

Keeping Visitors on Course from Whalebone Junction to the Whalehead Club

"What milepost?" They're usually the first two words upon any visitor's lips when seeking a dining establishment, beach access—even their own rental home. But finding your way along the Outer Banks wasn't always as simple as counting numbers on the side of the bypass. In fact, in the earliest days of tourism, little green signs weren't even necessary. Then again, neither were directions.

The Outer Banks' role as a resort destination predates the Civil War, when the well-to-do from the Albemarle region traveled by steamer or private vessel to Nags Head's sound side. The late unpleasantness postponed the tradition during the 1860s, but by 1870, eastern North Carolina upper-crusters were again summering in hotels and cottages that grew in the shadow of Jockey's Ridge. The first out-of-state visitors were mostly sportsmen, who hunkered down in hunting lodges to take advantage of the fine waterfowl available in winter months. And when the Wright brothers made Kitty Hawk famous in 1903—and again in 1908 and 1911—news-hungry journalists from around the country rented rooms in Manteo. In every case, they all came for a reason, with little chance to wander, and no way to get lost.

All that changed in the 1930s as bridges and roads finally allowed curious travelers to visit by automobile. After World War II, the businesses sprouting up along the Beach Road were eager to tout their locale to a new surge in curious vacationers. But that was not so easy on a strip of sand with few identifying features by which to navigate.

"Since there are no regular cross streets along the Dare beaches," explained Oscar Sanderlin, who chaired a special committee of the Dare Beaches Chamber of Commerce in 1950, "it is very difficult for strangers to find hotels or locate specific cottages."

Sanderlin's committee decided to erect signs every mile along the Beach Road, known then as Virginia Dare Trail—at the time the only north–south thoroughfare.

"These mile posts will serve as a substitute for street signs," continued Sanderlin, "so that residents as well as visitors can more easily find their way around."

Thus, an Outer Banks institution was born—the milepost marker.

According to late Outer Banks historian David Stick, the special committee "arranged for the Chamber to pay for the construction of twenty signs, each one containing the letters 'M.P.' and the mile number on both sides." At first, the signs were posted between only the Wright Memorial Bridge and the Roanoke Sound Bridge. They were installed by state highway workers in time for the 1950 summer season and featured "reflectorized material to make them visible at night."

Over coming years, businesses used the new signs in advertisements, directing visitors to their stores, motels and restaurants—occasionally even moving the markers closer to make their businesses easier to find. Nevertheless, the system worked well enough—until 1980, when new, larger signs began to replace the original mile markers along the Beach Road and to populate the newer 158 Bypass.

Suddenly, more than a few establishments were chagrined after the new markers went up when they learned the original markers weren't geographically accurate. (Especially hard-hit was the Milepost 11 Association, a federation of businesses that was shocked to discover they were much more in the vicinity of MP 10.) But most storefronts adapted. So did the visitors. And with time, the novelty, practicality and popularity of the mileposts led to their expansion down past South Nags Head all the way to Hatteras Village.

Today, the final marker is Milepost 72 near Lee Robinson General Store. They are especially helpful along Hatteras Island, where the national seashore keeps expanses of rolling dunes undeveloped. Often, a marker is the only way to remember or share the location of a sweet surf spot or a secluded stretch of beach.

In 2006, the Currituck Banks (now known as the Currituck Outer Banks) got in on the mile marker scene by erecting its own system—except

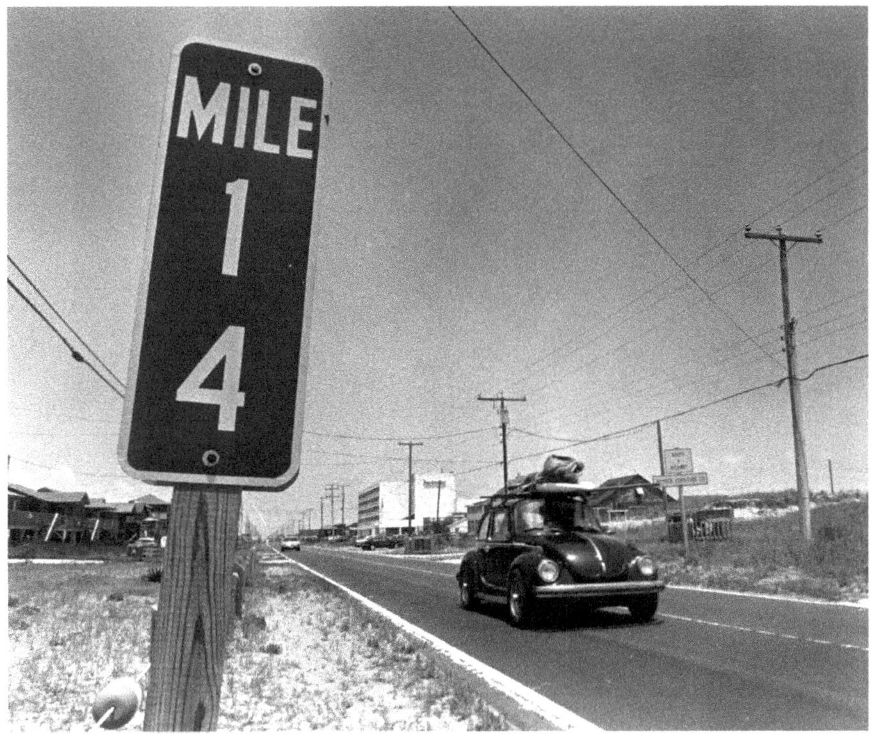

A green-and-white milepost marker on the Beach Road in Nags Head. *Drew C. Wilson Photo Collection, Outer Banks History Center, 1989.*

its starts at the Currituck–Dare County line, ascending in number all the way to Corolla and into the four-wheel-drive area. The county also opted for a more fashionable white-and-blue paint job instead of shiny, industrial green.

Ben Wood with the Currituck County Planning Department said officials have "generally found that the mile marker signs are not successful." (New numbers and hues can only confuse a weary traveler.) Instead, they have begun working on a "comprehensive wayfinding signage package." In 2015, the county began seeking bids to construct a number of signs for the Currituck Outer Banks, including directional, informational, beach access and orientation signage that "fosters safe travel for vehicular, bicycle and pedestrian traffic."

But down on what was referred to as the Dare Coast Beaches, mileposts are still highly functional sixty-five years later. In fact, today, you'll find markers every half mile to account for a more crowded bypass—and Nags Head's the Shoppes at Milepost 10.5, Kill Devil Hills' Milepost 6 Plaza and Kitty Hawk's Milepost 4.5 shops all attest to their economic power. And while a series of green metal signs may seem outdated in a modern age of talking apps and GPS systems, the milepost system is more than just nostalgia—it's a living, breathing part of Outer Banks life.

THE UNTOLD HISTORY OF THE 158 BYPASS

Have you ever seen the Outer Banks from the air? If you've not been adventuresome enough to take an air tour, perhaps you have viewed some aerial photos of this ribbon of sand. What stands out on the Northern Beaches—the seaside towns of Kitty Hawk, Kill Devil Hills and Nags Head—along North Carolina's Outer Banks is the ability to easily pick out the two north–south thoroughfares that carry natives and newcomers, vacationers, service workers and commercial trucks delivering food to restaurants, linens to hotels, bric-a-brac to trinket shops and bait to tackle stores.

To the east is the older, slimmer and slower Beach Road, and to the west is the newer, wider and faster bypass. These common designations simplify a complicated history of the highways. Names and numbers have changed over the years, while popular culture has endeared these streets in our hearts and collective vacation memories.

The history of the Beach Road is closely tied to the construction of two bridges—one built in 1927 connecting Roanoke Island and Nags Head, and the other linking Point Harbor at the southern tip of Currituck County to Kitty Hawk. The Roanoke Sound Bridge was the brainchild of Dare County commissioner Washington Baum, who had big plans for his native Roanoke Island, even though he faced opposition from his local constituents.

The northern span, the Wright Memorial Bridge, was started by the Kitty Hawk Company. Formed in 1929, the company's goals were to build a toll bridge over the Currituck Sound, to collect fees and to develop land in the

Kitty Hawk beach area—selling lots, building roads, and providing necessary infrastructure. The Kitty Hawk Company ran into financial difficulties while the bridge was still under construction and it was liquidated at a foreclosure sale, but a charter was granted to the Wright Memorial Bridge Company to finish the job.

The Wright Memorial Bridge opened for traffic on September 27, 1930, and less than two years later, a hard-surfaced road was built to connect the two bridges. North Carolina, which touted itself as "The Good Roads State," had an ambitious plan for all of its county seats to be connected by hard-surfaced roads. Under this same good roads initiative, the new Beach Road became part of a much larger Virginia Dare Trail that brought cars traveling east and west through the Albemarle region of North Carolina and north and south along the Dare Beaches, ending up in Manteo.

On early maps, the new Beach Road was shown as NC 345 and NC 34 before being upgrading to US 158 status. The thoroughfare was only two years old when it was washed out in Kitty Hawk by a September 1933 hurricane.

As more and more restaurants, juke joints and seaside hotels were built along the Beach Road, during the summer, this chief artery was getting clogged with summer traffic and it was slow going for those traveling from Kitty Hawk to Manteo or Hatteras Island.

In 1956, the State Highway Department announced it had $700,000 set aside for constructing an alternate US 158 to the west of the original, but if the necessary rights-of-way were not obtained in a timely fashion, the money would revert to other needed highway improvements in the Tar Heel State.

"The new road would carry US 158 from Wright Memorial Bridge through Jockey Ridge through to Whalebone, and would lie about 1,000 feet west or inland from the present road," reported the local newspaper, the *Coastland Times*. W.H. Rogers, an engineer with the State Highway Department, explained that the new site would "provide a location less affected by ocean storms and a road which would be able to handle beach season traffic with less congestion."

Bids for the job were opened on June 25, 1957, and by the close of the summer season, Raleigh's F.D. Cline Paving Company received an $800,000 contract to grade and pave the fifteen-mile stretch from Kitty Hawk to Whalebone Junction, while the job of removing buildings was awarded to Crouch Brothers out of Mooresville, North Carolina. The State Highway Commission worked with the local jurisdictions negotiating rights-of-way through the three beachside towns.

Creating a new highway along the Outer Banks would not only ease traffic on the overburdened Beach Road, but it would also provide new spaces for commercial development along its east and west sides. Enterprising citizens invested in road-front property. After the new highway's construction, new location names became part of the everyday Outer Banks lexicon. People vacationed or lived Oceanfront, Between the Highways or Westside.

On March 7, 1962, the Ash Wednesday Storm left its watery calling card along the Outer Banks and the Atlantic Seaboard when this "perfect storm" of high spring tides combined with a nasty coastal low-pressure system. The US 158 Bypass was front and center during the tempest when it was proved that because it was built on a raised roadbed, it was higher than its surroundings and was an impediment to the free flow of storm tides that made occasional visits to the windswept banks. The US 158 Bypass acted as a virtual dike and kept ocean water from making its way toward the sound.

Especially hard-hit was the Nags Head Historic Cottage District. Outer Banks native fisherman Jethro Midgett Sr. had been an outspoken adversary to the raised bypass. "The (expletive) never should have been put where it was because it blocks the ocean going to the sound," he told reporter Lawrence Maddry in 1962. "I told them about it, told them what it would do, but they built it anyway. A child would have known better." As a step toward a solution, a culvert was installed under the highway to allow the flow of flood tide.

Later that year, problems arose with slow-driving sightseers along the new ribbon of concrete. Under the headline "Minimum Speed for 158 Urged," an August 1962 front-page article in the *Coastland Times* reports on the town of Nags Head's dismay with drivers clogging up what was meant to be "a fast through route to Hatteras, Roanoke Island and other points, but that dawdling motorists were causing frequent traffic delays as well as an accident hazard." Officials wanted a forty-five-mile-per-hour minimum to keep travelers moving.

But in neighboring Kill Devil Hills, the board of commissioners did not agree. They were more amenable to a forty-mile-per-hour minimum because of busy intersections and the congested Avalon Beach section that flanked the US 158 Bypass near Milepost 6.

By the early 1980s, in order to give this additional and much relied upon thoroughfare a more appealing moniker, schoolchildren were enlisted to come up with a new name for the bypass. Over two hundred suggestions were made in the "Name the US 158 Bypass Contest," but the winning entry came from Heather Tolson of Kitty Hawk Elementary School. The

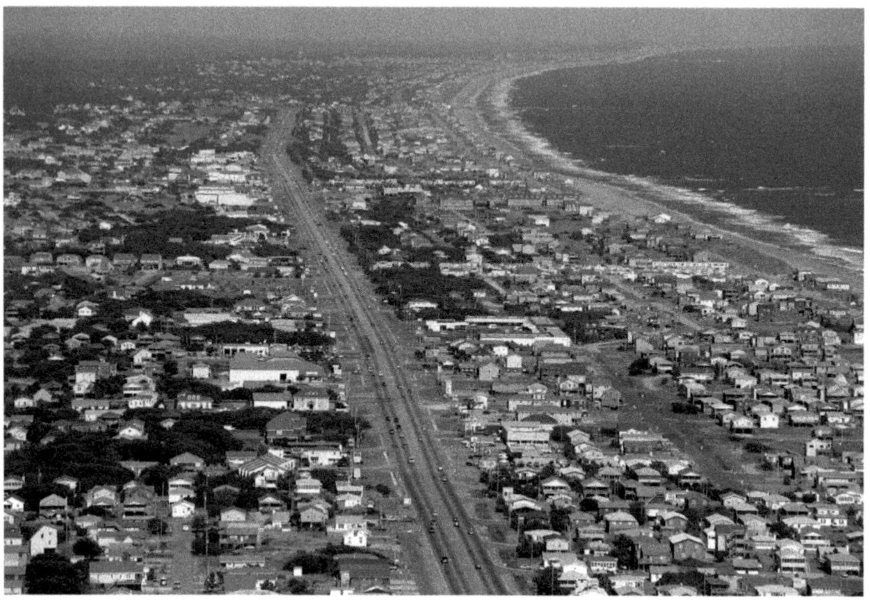

The US 158 Bypass in a view looking north near the Kill Devil Hills–Kitty Hawk town line. *Drew C. Wilson photograph. Collection of the photographer, 1998.*

sixth grader proposed the name Croatan Highway, after a location on Hatteras Island that made its way into history when it was carved on a tree as a message by Sir Walter Raleigh's 1587 colonists.

In order to keep up with the times *and* the flow of traffic, portions of the bypass were four-laned, or rather five-laned, in the '80s in order to ease congestion. The infamous French-Fry Alley in Kill Devil Hills was one of the areas where two additional traffic lanes were added, north- and southbound; but also included was a middle lane, a sort of free-for-all space used in preparation to make a left-hand turn. By moving over into the dual-direction lane to wait for a break in oncoming traffic in order to make a turn, drivers avoided stopping in a lane of moving vehicles.

Driving on the bypass during this era was a challenge indeed. Although the five-laning more or less modernized the road, it left the narrower stretches in a time warp. When the asphalt resumed to two lanes, it made for a maddening scene southbound as fast drivers went all out to make sure they were not stuck behind a slowpoke headed to Roanoke Island. Manteo High School students and nine-to-fivers jockeyed for position with unrelenting determination.

Robert H. Ross of Kitty Hawk expressed his concern in a letter to the editor: "As it exists, now, two lanes of traffic may be travelling side by side at 55 miles per hour only to suddenly realize that they must quickly funnel themselves into one lane." Ross contended that the entire road should have been expanded. He was right, and when additional funds became available, the whole bypass was widened.

Today, the bypass carries locals and vacationers to their various destinations and offer shoppers, gastronomes and the adventurous a host of shops, restaurants and recreational pursuits. It is quite a change from the two-lane alternate that was created sixty years ago.

FLAT TOP FOUNDATION

Avalon Beach Marks the Start of KDH as a Tourist Town—and the Structure for an Outer Banks Rental Market

The Outer Banks vacation rental business runs like an arms race. A world where developers and rental companies battle to outdo their neighbors, resulting in bigger and better homes full of high-tech convenience. Today, accommodations offer game rooms, wet bars, swimming pools—even in-home movie theaters. However, it wasn't always this way. In the beginning, modern convenience meant little more than four walls, a flat roof and a short walk to the water.

In a 1951 brochure for Avalon Beach, there is no discussion of granite countertops—"7 miles of concrete streets" is a firm enough sales pitch. Yet, according to the copy, "120 modern beach cottages have been built by individual purchasers and more are going up all the time."

Created during the surge of development following World War II, this tiny subdivision marked the start of Kill Devil Hills, our most populous tourist town. More than 1,100 modest fifty-by-one hundred-foot lots were already platted and offered for sale for second homes or investment properties. The down payment? A low $125, sometimes cheaper. Unlike today, developers didn't woo wealthy buyers as potential investors. Instead, they courted blue-collar families, writing introductory letters to shipyard workers from the Tidewater, Virginia area. Some eager realtors even delivered brochures personally.

"Every week or so my father went up to the Ford Motor Company in Norfolk or the shipyard in Newport News and put flyers on the windshields," recalls Tanya Young. Besides heading the Kill Devil Hills Historic Landmark

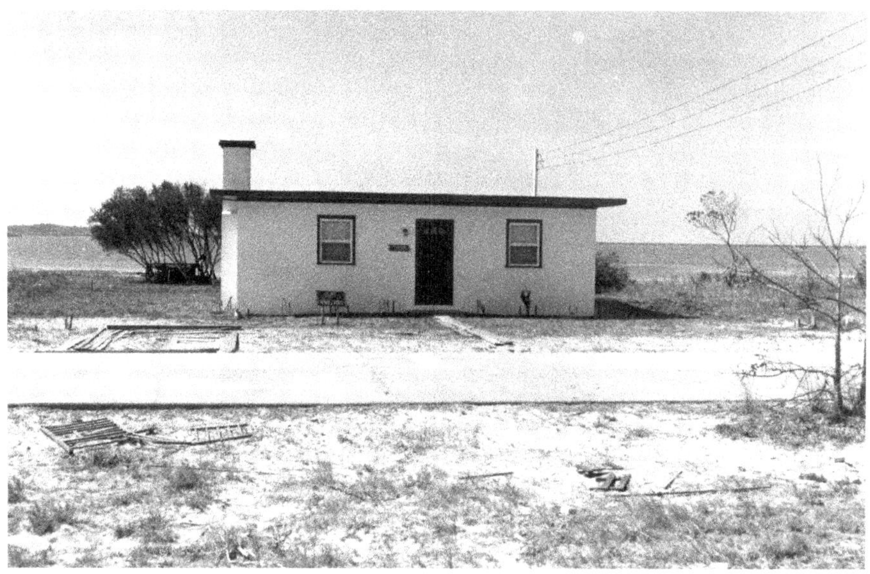

A modest flattop cottage on Kitty Hawk Bay in Avalon Beach. *Roger Meekins Collection, Outer Banks History Center, 1954.*

Commission, Young grew up in Avalon; in fact, her father, Robert Young, helped develop the neighborhood.

"That was the marketing," she continues. "It wasn't on the radio. It wasn't in the newspaper, he'd simply take those flyers and people would come down. Then he'd sell them a lot and take payments. It allowed those people who had steady income to have the opportunity to own a second home."

Now you know why streets in Avalon Beach bear the names of humble towns from Virginia and eastern North Carolina—Yorktown, Rocky Mount, Hampton, Newport News—instead of exotic tropical paradises.

The cottages were equally modest; all came with just two bedrooms and less than eight hundred square feet. Most had flat roofs. And all were made of concrete, which was a good insulator, keeping homes cool in the summer and warm in the winter. Screen porches and fireplaces sometimes helped regulate temperature.

Under the headline "Summer Cottages Sprouting Like Flowers in Early Spring," a lengthy article in the March 27, 1953 edition of the *Coastland Times* mentions several homes under construction in Kill Devil Hills and Kitty Hawk. One oceanside cottage by Portsmouth, Virginia's C.L. Kelly featured such luxuries as "a living room, kitchen, two bedrooms and a bath, the whole surrounded by a wide porch. It will have a flat roof."

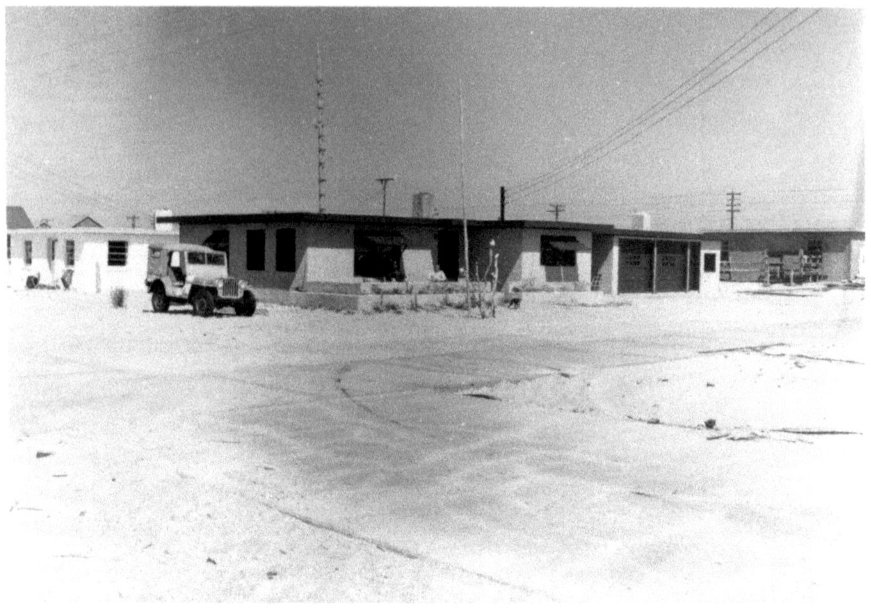

Flattop cottages were some of the first constructed in Avalon Beach. *Roger Meekins Collection, Outer Banks History Center, 1954.*

By 1969, the Robert Young and Associates rental catalog boasted dozens of options in the Avalon Beach neighborhood. An oceanfront model rented for a cool $150 a week, while farther from the water prices were as low as $65.

Today, the subdivision is defined by three east–west streets that run from the Beach Road to Bay Drive: Sportsman Drive (originally known as Kitty Hawk Drive), Avalon Drive and Durham Street, which run from the Beach Road to Bay Drive. Another east–west thoroughfare, Suffolk Street, connects Elizabeth City Street to down to Edenton Street. Highview Street—named for the ridge upon which it still stands—marks the center point. Still, while the streets sound familiar—and the parking area south of Avalon Pier looks like the same empty sandlot from a half century ago—the rest of the neighborhood has filled out considerably.

Instead of a sparse population of block structures and open space, you'll find rows of pilings from sound to sea. But take a bike ride some sunny afternoon—you can still spot a few cool, old-school squares. In fact, Ms. Young is happy to report that some are even on the historic registry. And while vintage selling points like "Formica countertops" and "knotty pine cabinets" may sound like antiquated amenities by our modern standards, those simple boxes contributed the most single important construction idea in the history of Outer Banks architecture—one that laid the very foundation for every luxury accommodation that goes up.

"Dad made it a moneymaking venture [for his clients]," says Young. "He said, 'Buy the lot and get it paid for, we'll build a house and rent it for you.' And that's how the rental market came into play."

THE NEW DEAL COMES TO THE COAST

Lasting and Not So Lasting Effects of Depression-Era Relief

On Inauguration Day, March 4, 1933, when Franklin Delano Roosevelt began his first term as president of the United States, the nation was in the midst of a global economic meltdown known as the Great Depression. Following the October 1929 stock market crash, banks failed, unemployment soared and the gross domestic product dropped over 20 percent. After campaigning on a platform of a "New Deal" for America, early in his administration, Roosevelt signed several acts into law designed to stabilize the economy and to put the jobless back to work. While the Outer Banks had recently become more accessible to the mainland and the outside world via the Wright Memorial Bridge, they were still chiefly undeveloped and sparsely populated. However, projects of that era found their way to Roanoke Island and the beaches. Some New Deal accomplishments are still visible, while others have been lost to time.

One of the most remarkable changes made during the New Deal era was a project of sand fixation along the coast. Dunes were built and grasses planted from Currituck Beach to Ocracoke. The endeavor was undertaken by both men from the transient camp in Nags Head and young men from Civilian Conservation Corps (CCC) camps on Roanoke Island and at Cape Hatteras.

The transients were put to work with special funds distributed to individual states from the Federal Emergency Relief Act (FERA). "It started off with FERA," explained Brent McKee, researcher for the Living New Deal, a U-Cal-Berkley-based program that documents and celebrates accomplishments of the New Deal. "It gave grants to states, and the states could do what they wanted."

Under the direction of Frank Stick, Camp Kitty Hawk was established in Nags Head in April 1934. Men were housed at Parkerson's, a white two-story building on the Beach Road. According to a report of relief activities in the state, "Two hundred able-bodied men were sent to this camp and were engaged in drift fence construction to combat beach erosion."

By June 8 that same year, under the headline "Kitty Hawk Transients Expect to Preserve Dare Co.'s Coastal Wonderland," Elizabeth City's *Independent* newspaper explained the task:

> *The process of dune building consists in the placing of sand fences parallel to the ocean, and at a distance of one hundred to two hundred feet from the high tide mark. The fence itself may be made of four to six-inch planks six to seven feet in length separated from two to three inches and buried in two feet of sand. Fencing should be placed in the relation to the ocean at or near the extreme edge of the zone of sand drift, which would normally be from four to six or eight feet from the tide mark, which not only affords a certain leeway for additional upbuilding if found necessary. If properly constructed and placed during the season of sand drift the fencing will be covered between the space of two weeks to two months.*

"The Reconstruction of Fort Raleigh" on Roanoke Island was a popular project at the site thought to be the original settlement of Sir Walter Raleigh's colonists in the 1580s. The men and boys of the FERA Transient Camps and the CCC built a palisade from native juniper logs around the sixteen-acre Fort Raleigh property, with two log buildings marking either side of the entrance. Another smaller palisade was constructed inside to represent the site of the 1587 colony.

Inside this smaller palisade, more log buildings were built to resemble structures of the colonists' time, although they were later proven historically inaccurate. These buildings functioned as part of the site, serving as a museum, bathrooms and a pump house. A chapel built from hand-hewn white cedar logs and topped with a thatched roof was especially memorable and was the setting for many Roanoke Island weddings. These improvements to Fort Raleigh greatly enhanced its appeal, and visitation grew tenfold, reaching thirty thousand in 1935.

In 1941, the National Park Service took over the Fort Raleigh site. Due to the fact that they didn't represent the time period interpreted by the park, the

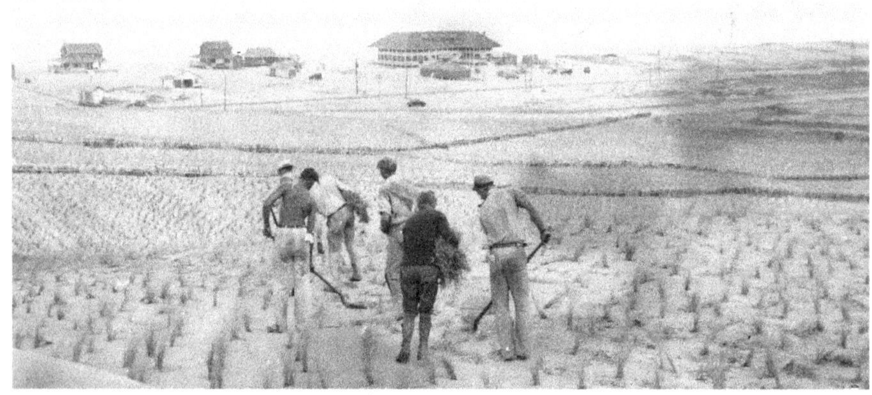

Men planting grasses to stabilize sand on Jockey's Ridge in Nags Head. The oceanfront hotel First Colony Inn is visible in the distance. *Clifton Murry Stetson Collection, Outer Banks History Center, 1937.*

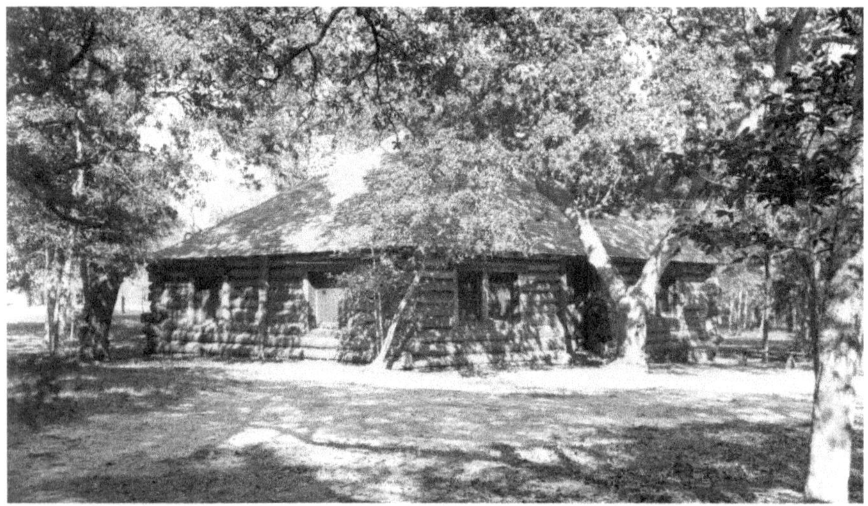

One of the log buildings constructed during the 1930s at the Fort Raleigh site on Roanoke Island. *Library of Congress, Prints & Photographs Division, Historic American Buildings Survey, NC, 28-MANT.V,1-B—1, circa 1939.*

log buildings were no longer maintained. Most were removed or destroyed after they fell into disrepair. The chapel was closed in 1950 and was razed in 1952. The last of the log buildings were removed in the 1960s.

Even America's longest-running outdoor drama, *The Lost Colony*, reaped the benefits of New Deal–era programs. During the first years of production, primary roles were filled with professional actors and actresses hired with funds from the Federal Theatre Project (FTP) of the Works Progress Administration (WPA). The inaugural 1937 season featured seven major parts played by professionals including Katherine Cale, in the role of Eleanor Dare, and Lillian Ashton, who was cast as Queen Elizabeth. Additionally, in the production seasons prior to World War II, boys from the CCC were hired as extras. These young men from eastern North Carolina debuted onstage playing native Algonquians in Paul Green's epic production.

However, three years before *The Lost Colony*'s debut, Martha Brothers Mathis began a theater group on Roanoke Island—the Elizabethan Players. Mathis had professional theater experience, and having lived in Pasquotank County as a child, she was familiar with the region's history. According to Cecelia Moore, author of *The Federal Theatre Project in the American South: The Carolina Playmakers and the Quest for American Drama,* Mathis started the troupe "with the help of a Civil Works Administration recreation grant and the promise of financial support from local promoters."

Prior to her arrival in 1934, Mathis corresponded with Elizabeth City newspaperman W.O. Saunders, who served on the Roanoke Historical Commission, and founding editor of Manteo's *Coastland Times*, D. Victor Meekins. The latter offered his sound-side cottage, Camp Contentment, as a place for Mathis and her husband to stay until more appropriate accommodations could be procured. These influential Albemarle men had interests in commemorating the 350th anniversary of Sir Walter Raleigh's colonists.

Mathis's goal was to create a dramatic ensemble to engage interested natives in presenting plays and pageants on historical topics. She and her husband financed part of the endeavor themselves, but without the assistance of local funds, the survival of the theater troupe was on the brink.

In 1936, the Federal Theatre Project stepped in and administered resources to employ Mathis as project supervisor and funded an additional three positions. The Elizabethan Players was one of nine theater groups in North Carolina, both black and white, supported by the FTP.

Mathis held playwriting classes and gave instruction in acting and voice. Dramas penned were written by natives about local subjects. They were

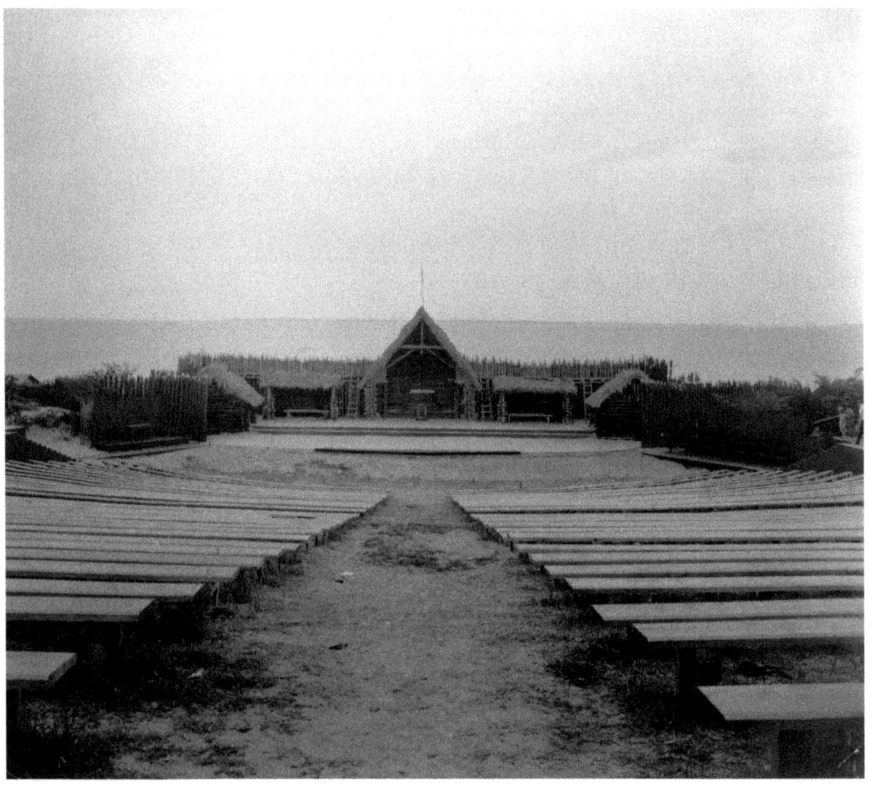

Waterside Theater, where *The Lost Colony* is performed, was built with WPA funds and WPA labor. *Collection of David Miller, 1937.*

presented in Manteo and Elizabeth City and although at times were not well attended, were still popular with audiences. This training in play production enabled many of the Elizabethan Players to land parts in *The Lost Colony*.

The town of Manteo gained at least three new structures financed in part by New Deal monies. In 1941, WPA funds aided in the construction of the Manteo Fire Station on County Street (now Budleigh Street). The Manteo Fire Department raised the balance due by organizing a series of fundraising dances. The downstairs of the station housed fire equipment while the upstairs served as town hall. The building was remodeled in 1977 when it received its Tudor makeover along with other facades in downtown Manteo. Today, it is privately owned.

The Community Building at the corner of US 64/264 and County Street was also built around this time and was the first permanent home for the

Dare County Public Library. The WPA provided money for the building and to hire a librarian. During World War II, USO dances were held there. In the 1970s and '80s, the building was home to the Dare County Tourist Bureau. Today it houses the Dare County Cooperative Extension Service.

A gymnasium, built in 1938, served the community for at least fifty years. Basketball games, physical education classes, teen dances and even auditions for *The Lost Colony* took place on its smooth wooden floors and under the large wooden eaves. The WPA gymnasium was torn down in 2013 in order to expand Manteo Elementary School, but not before a local split between education and preservation contingents.

How many New Deal–era buildings are still intact? "It's impossible to tell," says McKee. "There've been a lot demolished over the past eight decades, especially recently." He was contacted and requested to travel to Manteo to photograph, document and map the WPA gymnasium in the days prior to its demise. What if the call hadn't come? "There's a 50 percent chance it would've been lost to documentation," he says.

The Living New Deal has recorded and mapped over fifteen thousand structures and sites (including a handful in Dare County) with the help of volunteer field workers, including McKee and your author.

THE DEDICATION OF THE VIRGINIA DARE MEMORIAL BRIDGE

Our Place in Time

Eminentos, politicos and average Joes joined together for a great celebration on Friday, August 16, 2002—the dedication of the Virginia Dare Memorial Bridge, the four-lane span that connects Roanoke Island and mainland Dare County. The route is known as the 64/264 Bypass.

It was a great day for the region and a time to reflect on the past and the future. During my tenure in Dare, a new mid-county bridge was talked about, studied, planned and finally built. It was a process that took years! While it was under construction, the sight of the unfinished bridge—each time I arrived in Manns Harbor returning from Raleigh, Greenville and other points west—conjured up visions of improved travel and a shorter drive home. It was as if I could almost see my South Nags Head home from the mainland.

On dedication day, I came to the realization that the bridge was finished. The idea, the design, the construction—they were all complete! All that was left were the speeches, the cheers, the hand clapping and then the motorcade procession across the concrete ribbon over the tawny sound. History and traffic patterns had changed course.

Working at the Outer Banks History Center put me in contact with ephemera from other bridge dedications—the Lindsay C. Warren, William B. Umstead and Herbert C. Bonner Bridges (that's Alligator River, Manns Harbor and Oregon Inlet Bridges respectively). The Bonner Bridge was dedicated the year I was born, as was the Chesapeake Bay Bridge-Tunnel that connects Virginia Beach to the Eastern Shore. Yes, I associate my age with that of bridges I have traveled. The Umstead Bridge was dedicated in conjunction with the 1958 Pirate's Jamboree, a fact I discovered while researching an exhibit. I saw photos of Dare County pirates riding in convertibles and celebrating.

It was an honor to attend the Virginia Dare Memorial Bridge dedication. Truly, it was my day, my place in time, my bridge. The most inspiring observation made that festive day was the interaction of jubilant Dare Countians—young and old, from Hatteras Island and up the beach, Democrats and Republicans, all focused on the joy of the occasion. We were all giddy, proud and united.

The day was hot, not just hot, hotter'n heck. Few in the crowd had on appropriate hats to shade themselves from the wretched August sun. My companions and I sought shade by the side of the Roanoke Island Festival Park (RIFP) pickup truck, which was waiting in line to pull the *Elizabeth II*'s ship's boat, *Silver Chalice*, in the motorcade processional. We were far enough away that the speeches were only semi-audible, but we were treated to a breeze off the sound.

I thought for a moment about Eleanor White Dare, baby Virginia's mother. Was August 18, 1587, the day she gave birth to the first English child known to be born in America, as oppressively hot as this day? Additional thoughts of childbirth in the New World snapped me back to 2002.

Before too long, the speeches ended and the ribbon was cut and the motorcade was to proceed. We, employees from the Outer Banks History Center and RIFP, climbed into the back of the pickup. *The Lost Colony* choir climbed into the "chalice." Carroll Williams, head of maintenance at RIFP, started the truck. All cranked their engines.

Looking forward, I couldn't see Andy Griffith and Governor Michael Easley, who led the procession with their wives in one of Andy's antique autos. But I did see the back of Miss Barbara Hird's head protruding from the sunroof of a white limo as the acclaimed actress and principal of Elizabeth R and Co. rode into history.

As the crowd parted, the truck began to move, and we begin the wave. As we approached the bridge, people watched, took photos and waved. I heard at least two folks in the crowd call my name. I waved back. After passing the happy throng, the bridge began and I felt like a child at Christmas. The concrete was new; the sky was decorated with a complicated cloud structure. The procession ran in single file for a time, and then spread out into both lanes of the northern span, while on the southern side, cyclists, runners,

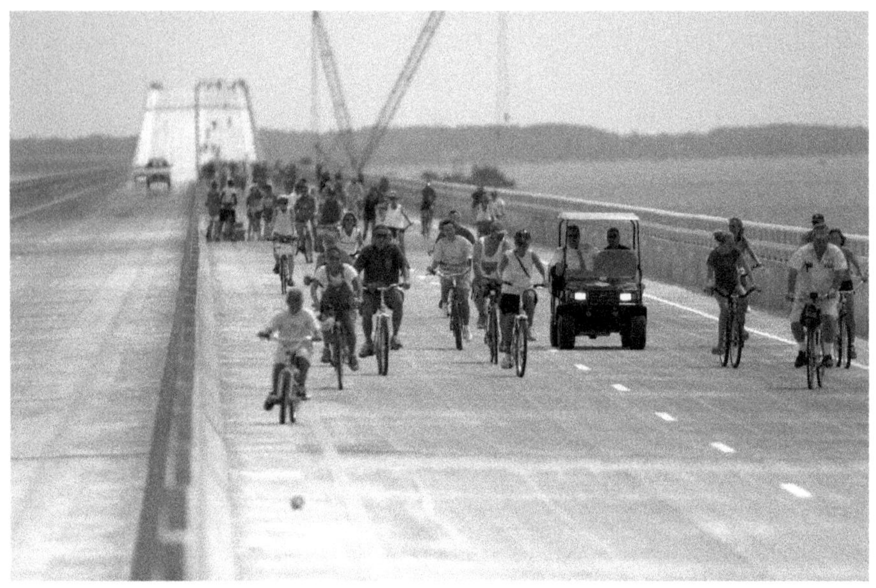

Cyclists peddling west on the south span of the Virginia Dare Memorial Bridge on dedication day. *Drew C. Wilson photograph. Collection of the photographer, 2002.*

walkers and skateboarders made their way to Manns Harbor. Boats were in the sound, and we waved to them.

After our wait in the mid-morning sun amid the pines and marshy surroundings, the feel of the breeze as we rode across the new bridge was exhilarating. Carroll pulled over at a water station set up along the route, lest his passengers wither in the heat.

Our entourage was passed by an official Town of Southern Shores delegation and some of us felt as though we had lost rank, but soon a group of Harley-Davidsons drove up alongside us. "What a contrast," exclaimed Suzanne Godley of RIFP, referring to the costumed *Lost Colony* choir in the wooden vessel and the engines and steel of the motorcycles. I snapped a photo, and we rode together for a while. At one time, we mingled with the brigade of antique autos. Virginia Tillett passed us in an old-timey car. All of us waved.

By the time we reached the peak of the bridge, the excitement of the excursion had also peaked. It *is* the longest bridge in the state. Quietly, we rode together, soaking in the beauty of our surroundings, contemplating the events just witnessed. A final burst of excitement was shared as we reach the end of the bridge. A small group had assembled at Manns

Harbor to greet the historic first passengers from the east side. And finally, we passed an assembly of Department of Transportation workers and, at Suzanne's suggestion, gave them a rousing round of applause.

That's pretty much the story. I had to write it all down to share with those who weren't there and for those not yet born. There will be other new bridges, and we will retire old bridges, but August 16, 2002, was our day, our place in time, our celebration.

PART V

SUNDRY TALES

HAIL TO THE CHIEFS

Remembering the Four Sitting Presidents Who've Paid Us a Visit

If you lived on the Outer Banks in 2003, you remember the First Flight Centennial Celebration. All year long, organizers hustled and hyped to build a special event that would commemorate the Wright brothers' monumental achievement on the Outer Banks—and draw aviation enthusiasts from all over the world. On December 17, hundreds of fans braved a torrential downpour to pay tribute to the triumph of man over gravity. In return, they got to witness a replica 1903 flyer take to the air, rub elbows with celebrity aviators from John Glenn to John Travolta, plus enjoy a special visit from the forty-third president of the United States, George W. Bush.

As the program administrator of the First Flight Centennial Commission, Kim Sawyer still remembers receiving her "4:00 a.m. phone call" from the Secret Service. "They needed more umbrellas," she deadpans. "So we got some at Walmart."

Bush would bail before the end of the ceremony. And while some press outlets reported he was the first sitting U.S. president to visit the Outer Banks, at least three other "leaders of the free world" set foot on our sandy soil: one for work, one for fun, one for a bit of both.

President James Monroe became the first chief executive to tour the region—then known only as "the sand banks"—in April 1819. When he arrived aboard the steamer *Albemarle*, his goal was to survey the recently closed Roanoke Inlet located south of Jockey's Ridge. Back then, the nation was barely forty years old, so maintaining a route to the ocean was critical to

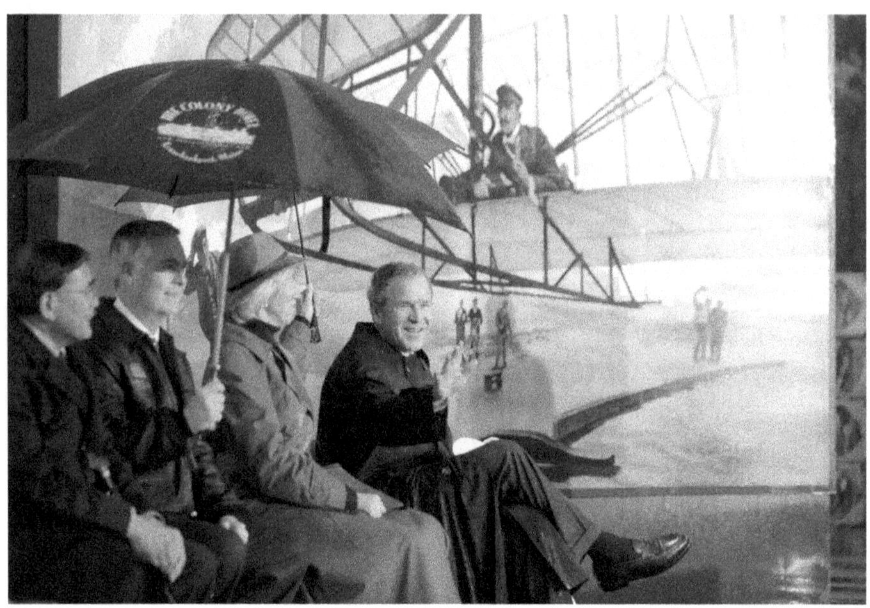

President George W. Bush at the Centennial of Flight Celebration at the Wright Brothers National Memorial. He is joined by (*right to left*) Gail Norton, U.S. Secretary of the Interior; Mike Easley, Governor of North Carolina; and Norman Mineta, U.S. Transportation Secretary. *Courtesy of the George W. Bush Presidential Library and Museum. White House Photo by Paul Morse, 2003.*

the development of the United States and North Carolina. But Monroe still made time for some sightseeing, coming ashore on Roanoke Island to view the site of Sir Walter Raleigh's ill-fated English colony.

It would be almost seventy-five years before the next president would pay a visit—or in this case, several. Grover Cleveland doesn't just hold the distinction of being the only U.S. president to serve two non-consecutive terms (1885–1889 and 1893–1897), he's also the Outer Banks' official "tourist-in-chief," making multiple trips to enjoy the abundant hunting and fishing opportunities.

In the days before I-95, D.C.'s ambassadors rode down on government lighthouse tenders, vessels that worked their way along the nation's waterways taking supplies to the far-flung outposts where the navigational beacons aided mariners in their journeys. Roanoke Island native Miles Creef's great-grandfather John Shannon was a keeper at the Bodie Island Lighthouse from 1887 to 1897, and apparently played host to Cleveland on one of his trips to Bodie Island—at least according to family lore. "The president came on a lighthouse tour and [John Shannon] took him hunting in the lighthouse ponds," recalls the Wanchese waterman with his customary grin. "That was always the story told to me by my momma."

Still, one might argue Franklin Delano Roosevelt contributed the most to the Outer Banks, as his New Deal built the dunes that line NC 12, created ditches to eradicate mosquitoes and funded the production of *The Lost Colony*. In 1937, FDR got to see the results firsthand, as he marked the 350th anniversary of the birth of Virginia Dare—the first known child born to English parents in America and namesake of Dare County—by attending the outdoor drama in its inaugural year.

In his memoir, *My Boyhood at the Beach,* George Spence recalls seeing Roosevelt in Nags Head's historic Buchanan cottage:

> *A ramp had been built in order to help him walk up onto the porch and an oak chair was carried inside for him to sit in. I remember sometime after lunch a friend and I went to the beach to see if we could get another*

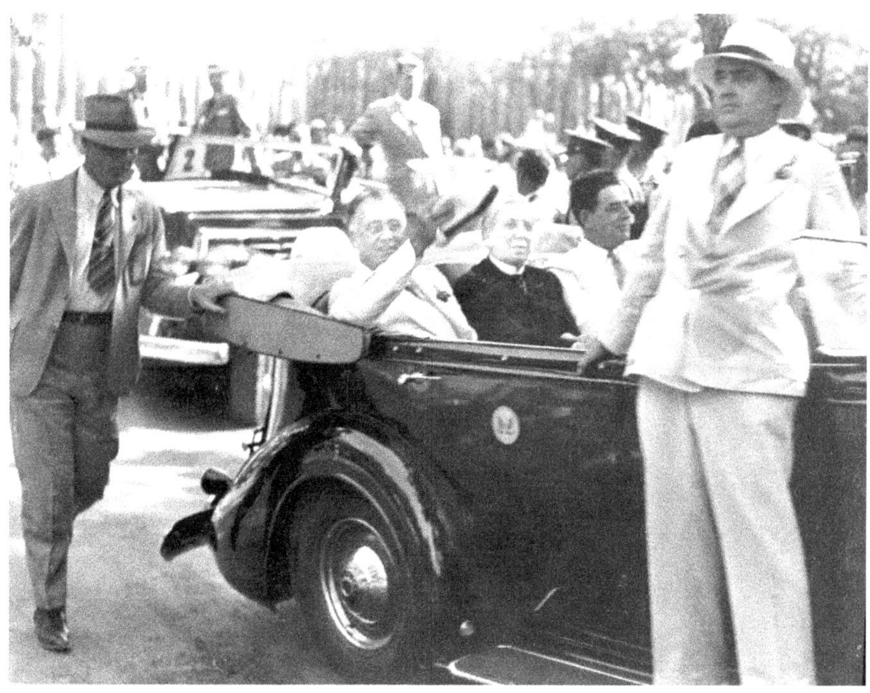

President Franklin D. Roosevelt gives a wave of his hat upon arrival at Waterside Theater to see Paul Green's outdoor drama *The Lost Colony*. Seated next to Roosevelt are North Carolina governor Clyde B. Hoey and Congressman Lindsay C. Warren. *Conservation and Development Department, Travel and Tourism photo files, North Carolina State Archives*, 1937.

> *glimpse of the president.... The president was seated in his chair on the porch looking out on the ocean. There were several Secret Service agents standing guard on the porch and out on the sand around the cottage and out toward the ocean. We obviously didn't dare go close.*

Like Bush, Roosevelt made his own quick exit. After attending *The Lost Colony*, he took a stealth trip back to Elizabeth City through the sultry Albemarle evening, arriving before midnight to board his private presidential train car for the trip back to Washington. According to history, we'll get another presidential visit from the White House inside fifty years, to salute our fabled history, take in a show or perhaps just relax on the beach. Maybe the next chief executive will show off his or her independent streak and stay a little bit longer.

LOCAL LAYOVER

The Outer Banks Didn't Just Give Birth to Human Flight—They Helped Deliver Commercial Aviation

December 17, 1903. On that cold and blustery day at Kitty Hawk, the Wright brothers ushered the modern world into the age of aviation with four successful flights. They sent a telegram to their father in Dayton, Ohio, announcing their accomplishment and headed home for Christmas. At first, the invention of flying was seen as a modern miracle. But within twenty years, riding on planes would become routine, and—once more—the Outer Banks would play a role when international passenger and mail service began between Key West, Florida, and Havana, Cuba, and Manteo became a stopover for seaplanes.

The hour-long flight was a major improvement over the eight-hour boat trip. Aeromarine West Indies Airways Inc. had a fleet of six seaplanes—chiefly converted Navy aircraft reconditioned following World War I. The flying boats had 104-foot wing spans and were powered by two 400-horsepower Liberty engines and, as the *New York Herald* reported, were "luxuriously equipped in mahogany and silver." Eleven or twelve passengers (accounts vary) flew with a crew of three. Passengers were able to take the "Highball Express" as it was dubbed, to escape the Prohibition-encumbered States and go party in "wet" Cuba.

The first Key West–Havana mail flight was scheduled for November 1, 1920, but as a precursory test run, Aeromarine's executives, their spouses and reporters from New York's *Evening Post* and *Times* newspapers traveled from the Big Apple to Key West. The planes enjoyed a sendoff from the Columbia Yacht Club on October 23 before soaring out over the Hudson River.

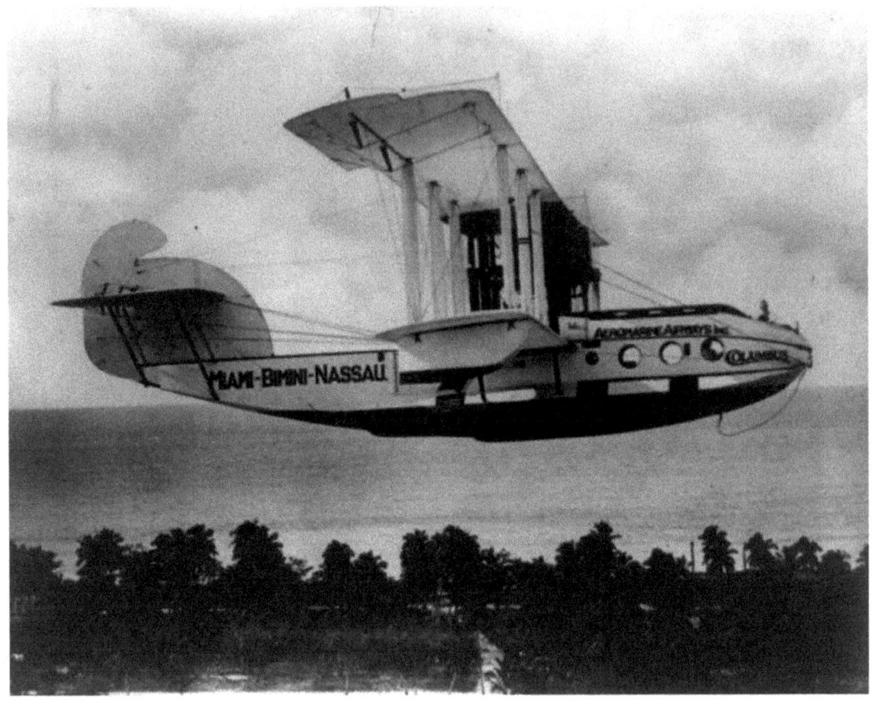

Aeromarine flights often used Manteo as a stopover on trips from the northeast to the Caribbean. This flight to Bimini was dubbed the Highball Express since it flew passengers to territories not restricted by America's prohibition laws. *Courtesy Library of Congress Prints and Photographs Division, 1922.*

Due to its location, as well as its historical draw, Manteo was a stopover point for the *Pinta* and *Santa Maria*. The flying boats landed in the sound beside Roanoke Island on October 25 and were met by a "white-haired sun-browned fisherman" who guided his skiff out to bring the air travelers ashore. Manteo's busy wharves attracted watercraft of all sizes, but gas-powered motors were not yet commonplace. Wilmington's *Morning Star* reported, "Gasoline happened to be at a premium," and it took the rest of the afternoon and part of the next day to fill the seaplanes to capacity.

Overnight accommodations were arranged at the Tranquil House, and the sojourners' belongings were collected at the dock and loaded into "extraordinary little carts made by the inhabitants [of the island] with two great wheels, one on either side and drawn by oxen." The entourage meandered to the inn, "up the narrow white sanded streets" and "along uneven grass grown sidewalks beneath the ancient trees," where the travelers made the way to their rooms by means of light cast by candles and oil lamps.

The following day, *Santa Maria* and *Pinta* caused such a ruckus that according to the newspaper, "Dare County Superior Court…was really obliged to give a recess so that everybody might be present to observe the departure of the planes." It wasn't just those with courthouse business who witnessed history; folks showed up from across the county, and "the wharves were literally packed with people."

Three local women were lucky enough to gain berth on the seaplanes for the next stint in the journey. Mabel Evans, Dare County superintendent of public instruction, chaperoned Louise Davenport, fifteen, and Augusta Peele, seventeen, on the flight down to Southport, North Carolina, on the Brunswick County coast. After a brief stay, the ladies took the train to Wilmington to start their trip home, taking with them hearts full of memories and travel tales to share back on Roanoke Island.

The second visit by an Aeromarine plane was in December 1920, when *Balboa*, on a flight between New York and Miami, stopped in Manteo for gas. Its large tank was filled when a careless crew member ditched a cigarette in Shallowbag Bay, igniting waterborne fuel that had spilled overboard. According to the *Independent*, "For a time, the waterfront of Manteo was threatened by the fire, and many boats lying in the harbor had to be towed to safety." Fortunately, the Coast Guard cutter *Dare* was stationed at Manteo and boatswains mate George P. Midgett, engineman first class W.B. Midgett and electrician E. Midgett aided in fighting the flames and saved the flying boat from complete ruin. The mishap caused the aircraft to remain on Roanoke Island until proper repairs could be made.

Ponce de Leon stopped at Manteo to take on oil during a flight from New York in mid-February 1921. All was swell until its attempted takeoff, when the seaplane clipped the rigging of a schooner anchored nearby. Afterward, it was decided that flying boats should be towed to deeper water before they commenced their ascents.

Aeromarine West Indies Airways reorganized as Aeromarine Airways in early 1921 and expanded service to the Bahamas and Bimini and runs between New York City, Atlantic City, points on Long Island and Lake George, New York. The company ceased operations in 1924 after the Post Office Department froze government contracts. The seaplanes' visits to Manteo, in the days before paved roads and bridges, are interesting footnotes from aviation's early days and illustrate the leading edge of what's become an air travel tradition, as modern planes continue to stopover in Manteo for southern hospitality and fine coastal fare.

THREE HUNDRED SIXTY-ONE YEARS IN THE MAKING

The Second Beheading of Sir Walter Raleigh

Sir Walter Raleigh, courtier to Queen Elizabeth I, poet and adventurer, looms in eastern North Carolina. The state capital is named for him, as was a fort on the north end of Roanoke Island where in the late 1500s a series of settlements were attempted so that the English might get a foothold in the New World. However, for a time, a likeness of Sir Walter loomed very large over downtown Manteo.

This rendering was in the form of a twenty-four-foot, fifteen-thousand-pound wooden sculpture created by artist Robert K. Harniman as part of the American Revolution bicentennial observance in North Carolina. He took ten months to carve the statue with chain saws and chisels. His studio was the North Hills Fashion Mall in Raleigh, where shoppers could watch the artist at work.

Harniman was in his twenties at the time he created the mammoth sculpture. He called himself "The Tree Carver" and claimed he had "learned to use a chain saw like a surgeon's scalpel." His medium was a five-hundred-year-old cypress tree found in the Tar River Swamp in Pitt County with the help of aerial searches performed by the Weyerhaeuser Company. The tree trunk had a Y-shape and was turned over to form the legs of Sir Walter Raleigh.

The statue was billed as the largest moveable wooden sculpture in the world, and as part of the bicentennial observance, the statue toured North Carolina, making its way as far west as Asheville. But after that, no one wanted him. Jule Burrus, who was a Manteo commissioner at that

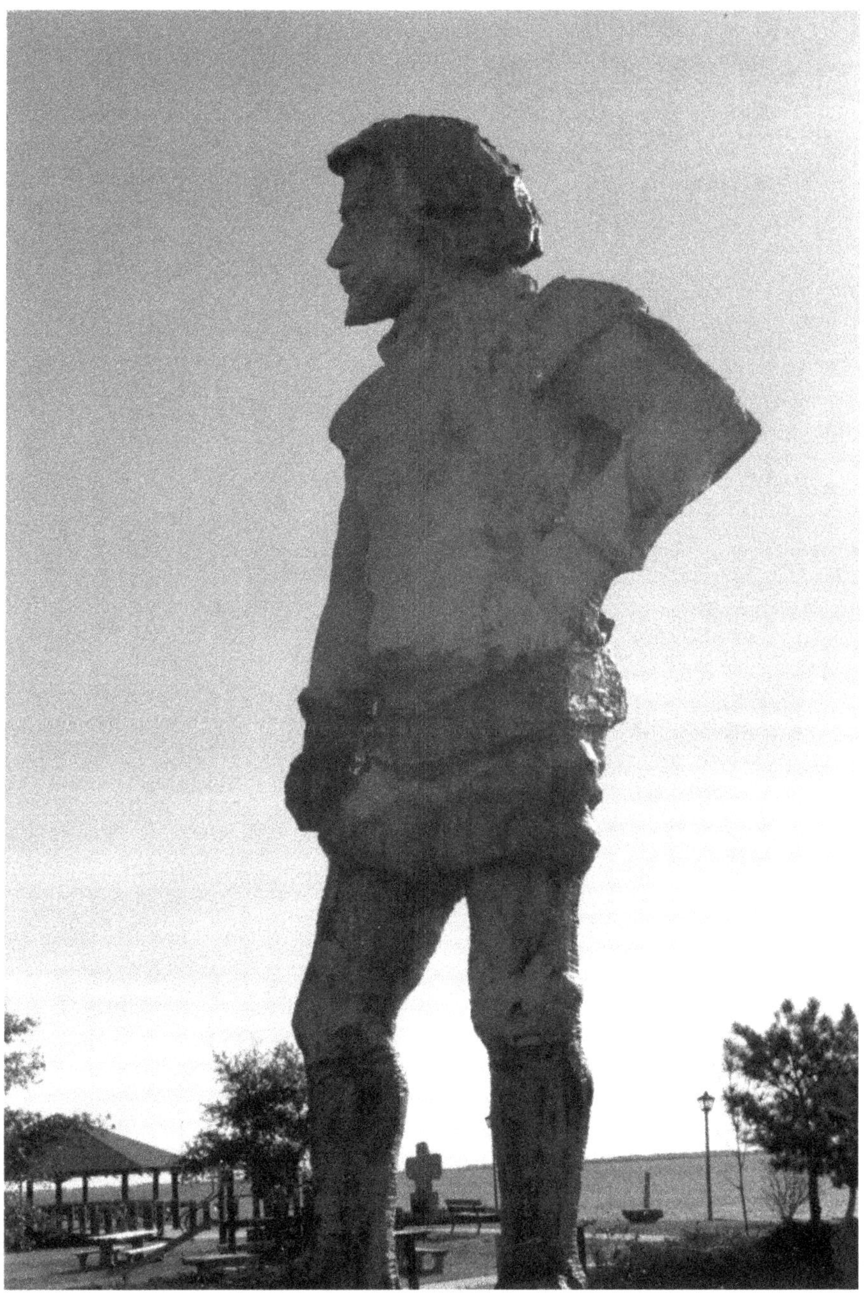

The wooden Sir Walter Raleigh statue stands watch over downtown Manteo. *Collection of the author, 1988.*

time, knew of the statue's plight and enlisted the help of Lynda Midgette. "Nobody wanted it and Jule found out about it. It would be perfect here." So Midgette, working with the Manteo Woman's Club, raised money through private and business donations to bring the statue to Manteo. "I can't remember how much money it was. It could've been 1,500 or 5,000 dollars. It [the statue] came in on a flatbed truck and was lifted in place with a crane."

So, the wooden sculpture of Sir Walter Raleigh found a home at the south end of Queen Elizabeth Street in Manteo, where for a dozen years its quizzical gaze looked down upon the county seat of Dare. "He was oddly proportioned—a wee bit short in the legs," recalled Suzanne Godley, former Manteo commissioner. Some found the statue a charming addition to the Manteo waterfront, while others thought it an eyesore.

Steve Brumfield of Manteo Booksellers recounted, "When the bookshop first opened you could look directly across the parking lot and see the statue. No buildings blocked the way as they do now. Customers would come in asking why there was a statue of Paul Bunyan on the waterfront!"

According to John F. Wilson IV, who served as mayor during the tenure of the Sir Walter Raleigh statue, "Tourists would send me dollars to put in the Remove Sir Walter Raleigh Statue Fund."

But time and elements took their toll on the sculpture. The once majestic piece of cypress began to rot. Venturesome woodpeckers began to look to the Sir Walter Raleigh statue as a source of food. Manteo officials decided to take the statue down for safety reasons, and that is when the sentimentality of the Sir Walter Raleigh statue hit home. Midgette recalls that day: "I was going to the post office and I saw James [McLease] on top of him with a chain saw. By the time I got there he had already been decapitated." Most folks found great irony in this because the real Sir Walter Raleigh was beheaded by James I in 1618.

Steve Brumfield was present when a town truck pulled the statue over: "When it hit the ground it broke into many pieces…because of the crudeness of the carving no part of the statue was recognizable as any particular piece once it had been separated from the statue as a whole. I can tell you that for certain because I looked closely at the various pieces once the statue was on the ground."

Manteo officials gladly allowed people to take pieces of the statue as mementoes. Midgette was awarded the Sir Walter Raleigh statue head. However, en route to her home, it toppled from the back of the truck and broke into pieces. Midgette had local carver Nick Sapone create waterfowl from the pieces, which are still on display in her home. She shared some couplets from a poem she wrote to memorialize the events:

As they rounded the bend
On the way to North End
He came to an end
Not fitting for him

Although the statue is gone, it still lives on in memory, photographs and verse.

ESCARGOT INVASION

How One Man's Entrepreneurial Idea Became a Sticky Situation

Invasive species and their impacts are nothing new to the Outer Banks. Lionfish pillage offshore wrecks. Red foxes raid hen houses from sound to shore. Gypsy moth caterpillars digest native trees. But there's one creepy foreign creature you've probably never noticed—much less considered. A form of edible livestock small and slow enough to stay out of sight for the past thirty years: *Cornu aspersa*. You might know it better as the European brown garden snail or—if you're an adventurous eater—escargot.

Well before French chefs smothered this delicacy in garlic and butter, humans consumed snails in many forms. In fact, shells of these terrestrial gastropods often show up in prehistoric middens, which are more or less the trash heaps of our earliest ancestors. And raising snails for food, otherwise known as heliciculture, is a practice that dates back to ancient times. Romans reportedly raised them in pens and fed them milk and wine to plump them up for their plates. But these particular snails were never found in North America until the 1850s—likely introduced by the French—where they quickly earned a reputation as pests among farmers, thanks to a penchant for devouring leafy greens.

In 1987, an Outer Banks entrepreneur decided to try propagating them for a burgeoning escargot business, hoping area restaurants would serve them to upper-crust epicureans and gastronomes. The Outer Banks were much less developed a quarter century ago. Even Kill Devil Hills remained relatively rural. He chose a nondescript spot in between the highways just

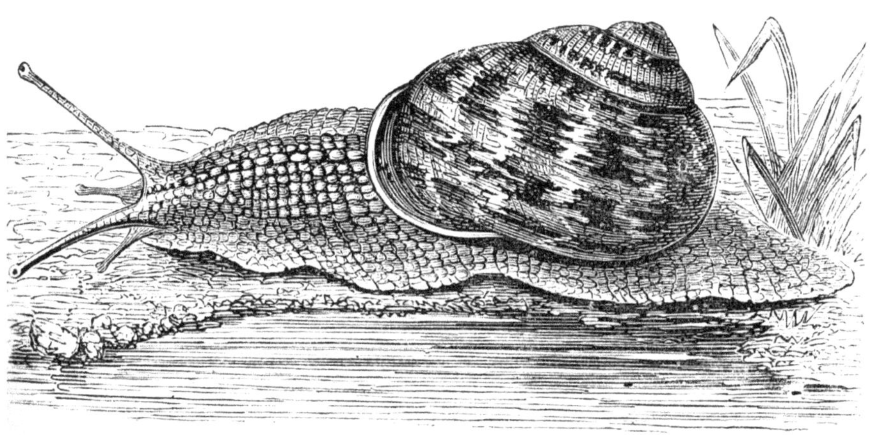

The garden snail, *Helix aspera*, from a nineteenth-century text. While known by that taxonomic name for two centuries, at the end of the twentieth century, it was reclassified and is now known as *Cornu aspersum*. *From* The Ocean World: Being a Description of the Sea, and Its Living Inhabitants. *London: Chapman & Hall. 1869.*

south of the Wright Brothers Memorial and raised the shelled delicacies in a small greenhouse shed.

The only trouble was that after a particularly hard blow, the structure failed and snails got loose. It turns out that the area's relatively mild temperatures and humid conditions were especially suited for the new fauna, which began to reproduce naturally in the wild.

Suddenly, a fun idea for foodies became a serious matter for North Carolina's economy, which faced a potential threat to the state's lucrative agriculture industry. Should sticky snails attach themselves to old boards or beach chairs and become transported inland, they might wreak real havoc among farmers' cash crops. According to David Pearce, a plant-pest specialist with the North Carolina Department of Agriculture, the species is so destructive the effects "can be catastrophic."

Officials quickly moved in. They began exterminating the shelled intruders and believed the eradication efforts were successful. However, when they checked again in the 1995, three hundred snails were found. In 1999, the *Coastland Times* reported that if the snail problem was not eliminated, "other states could put restrictions on North Carolina exports that could possibly be carriers of the snails, and that would mean increased costs to nursery operations, sod growers and other agricultural businesses."

So, the agents swept back in. To this day, they still visit the neighborhood where the snail farm originated, to poke around and make sure they haven't crawled too far out of bounds.

While agents first tried methods such as molluscicides and manually killing the pests to keep the snail's numbers down in the past, Pearce explains that currently, "The biggest objective is to contain the snail and keep it from spreading." And so, they continue to monitor the land that occupies the former snail farm.

According to a report by the North Carolina Department of Agriculture and Consumer Services, in 2011 an integrated pest management (IPM) strategy was initiated that involved "using a more environmentally friendly product, systematically killing snails during periodical inspections and by raising awareness in the community." The new IPM has brought the shelled nuisance numbers down. Every other week, snail collection sites are checked—so often that residents and neighbors recognize the state pest specialists.

As Pearce says, "They call us the snail police."

BURNING RUBBER

How a Huge Stash of Tires Left Locals and Law Enforcement Dazed and Confused

Part of the lure and the lore of the sea is its mystery. The great Atlantic is always taking and giving with the ebb and flow of the tide. Anyone familiar with the Beachcomber Museum's collection of seashells, driftwood and assorted bottles amassed by Nags Head's legendary glass-gather—Nelly Myrtle Pridgen—can attest to the variety of treasures and trinkets that find their way to the sand. But even Ms. Pridgen would've been blown away by the tons of tar-like jetsam that washed up on the Outer Banks in the late '70s. The stuff was not oil. Nor was it petroleum-based. But, man, was it sticky.

Under the headline "More Dope Floats Up on Beaches," the *Coastland Times* of October 25, 1979, reported that "a total of 36 inner tubes packed with Mideast hashish [were] recovered from Duck to Ocracoke." To this date, it remains one of the largest drug seizures in Outer Banks history—totaling an estimated $3 million. But it wasn't just the size that made the find so amazing, but the packing. The illegal drug, derived from the resin of marijuana buds, was pressed into a brick or block shape, placed into plastic bags and then hidden inside truck tire inner tubes.

Officials floated theories as to how the suspicious packages arrived. Most speculated that one of the parties involved in a boat-to-boat drug deal rendezvous had failed to pick up his haul at a designated time and place so the drugs were set to sea. At that time, U.S. Customs officials were aware that drugs were being trafficked into the region by boat.

A 1976 newspaper article notes, "Isolated areas such as Sandbridge, Back Bay, the Outer Banks of North Carolina and Accomac on Virginia's Eastern Shore are known targets of smugglers."

Following the initial find, an air search was conducted and law enforcement from the State Bureau of Investigation, National Park Service, Dare County Sheriff's Department and the Coast Guard were brought in to try to locate the waterborne narcotics.

Sol Rose, a recreational boater from Franklin, Virginia, also retrieved three inner tubes he found floating five miles out to sea. Several more packages were found adrift in Hatteras Inlet. All that booty was turned over to the U.S. Customs Service, but a spokesman for the SBI thought "it was very probable that a portion of the contraband found its way into the hands of private citizens in the area."

Good hunch. One longtime Outer Banks resident, "William M.," who asked that we not reveal more of his identity, remembers first seeing the contraband at a keg party back in his younger and blonder days—and still smelling it elsewhere for years—as more supply trickled in one tire at a time. In fact, into the mid-80s, for years, an abundance of inexpensive hash remained available to partaking carpenters, plumbers and drywallers; cooks, waitresses and busboys; artists, musicians and fishermen; hotel clerks, real estate agents and general ne'er-do-wells.

"Fishermen were picking it up in their nets," Mr. M. suggests. "It was the fishermen bringing it in, even if it was by mistake."

All of them soon found the biggest mistake was smoking the stuff. Not because it killed brain cells, but because one large inhale filled lungs with a thick acrid fume that tasted like smoldering rubber. But enterprising Bankers soon found a solution: instead of sparking it up, they swallowed it whole. (Keep in mind the spirit of the time: Cheech and Chong were scoring big at the box office with movies such as their 1978 cult stoner classic, *Up in Smoke*. And the whole country laughed at *Saturday Night Live* skits laced with drug innuendoes.)

It was all funny until 1982, when John Belushi was found dead from a mixture of cocaine and heroin. That same year, First Lady Nancy Reagan challenged the nation's youth to "Just Say No," sparking a thirty-year trend of tougher laws. At least until modern times, where twenty-four states and the District of Columbia all have some form of legal cannabis, be it for pharmaceutical therapy or just plain fun. Just remember: none of those states are North Carolina. And none of the recreational uses include beach-driving.

PART VI

CAPRICIOUS SEAS

SHIP ASHORE

The Shining Star Betelgeuse *Becomes a Hatteras Island Attraction*

It was a dark and stormy night—no, no, really it was—when the Liberty ship *Betelgeuse* came ashore at Rodanthe, January 17, 1976. A tugboat was leading the 453-foot, 6,500-ton ship on a journey from the Philadelphia Navy Yard to Brownsville, Texas, when high seas and treacherous winds brought both vessels in danger of beaching. The tug captain ordered the towline released, and *Betelgeuse* wound up stranded in the sand near Salvo, tilted with a jaunty 10 percent list. The "Goose," as it was known, was property of the Luria Brothers Company of Brownsville, who had purchased the hulk of recyclable iron from the federal government for a cool $200,000. It would be cut into pieces and sold for scrap value.

While ashore, the wreck brought people out on the beach to see the curious sight. Mac Midgett, a young Hatterasman, full of promise as well as a good bit of spunk, affixed a line to the stranded vessel and fastened it to an anchor on the beach. Midgett claimed that by old maritime law, rights of a lost vessel were given to the first who made a claim to it. This later proved untrue but drew attention to the bold and sprightly actions of the bearded man who would later become a successful businessman, community leader and Dare County commissioner. (Fact: it was due to Midgett's persistence that the toll was removed on telephone calls between Hatteras Island and the northern beaches.)

So, the bleak, gray, stranded *Betelgeuse*—named for a bright red star visible in the constellation Orion—became somewhat of a local attraction that winter. Radio station WOBR reported live from the scene that Midgett was keeping watch on the *Betelgeuse* from his "four-wheel drive, rust-spotted pickup truck." A Coast Guard spokesman said that it was "up to the owners of the ship to get her unbeached."

Built in California, it began its career in 1944 as the SS *Columbia Victory* and worked as a Merchant Marine vessel in the Pacific. Following World War II, the ship became part of the Maritime Reserve Fleet until it was purchased by Uncle Sam and was made ready for service in his Navy.

In 1952, the ship was commissioned with its new name, USS *Betelgeuse*. Cargo ships as a class were given names of celestial bodies. After making supply runs to the Caribbean and Mediterranean, it was refitted in order to carry Polaris missiles and plied the Atlantic to Scotland and Spain.

The ship became something of an offseason attraction. Everyone wanted to see the aging hulk that was one of the last cargo vessels used by the U.S. Navy. Folks from the tri-village area, from up and down the beach and even from out of state trekked over the dunes to see the behemoth.

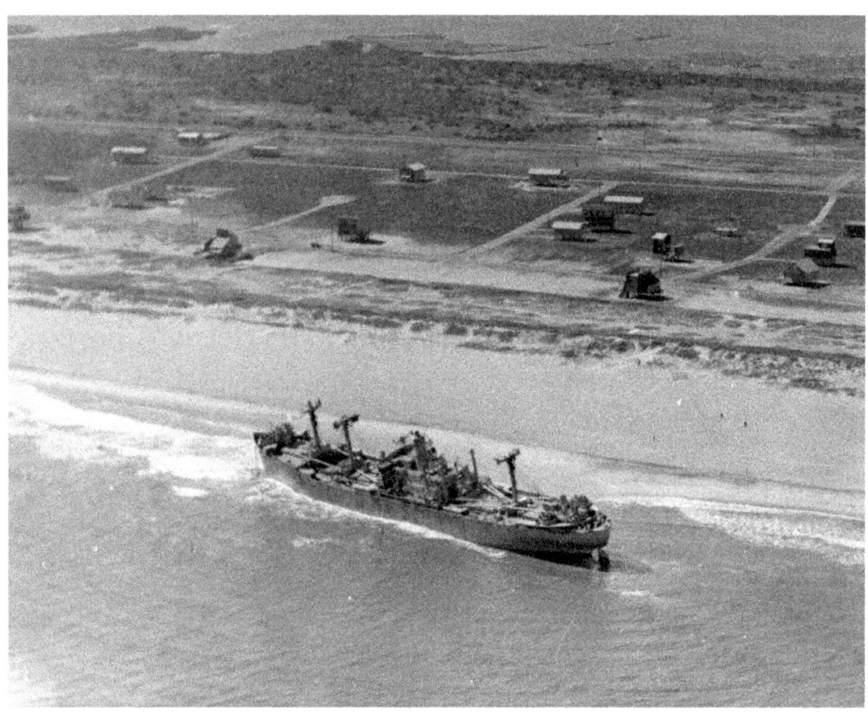

Betelgeuse grounded onshore at Salvo after breaking loose while under tow. *Aycock Brown Collection, Outer Banks History Center, 1976.*

The *Coastland Times* covered the incident and even polled weekend sightseers, asking them, "If you were in charge, what would you do with the *Betelgeuse*?" Creative responses included converting it into a floating condominium or a restaurant. Others suggested charging a fee for viewing.

A month following the stranding of *Betelgeuse*, Murphy-Pacific, a West Coast salvage firm, showed up with a barge laden with equipment. Mac Midgett thought his claim was over when he learned the *Betelgeuse*'s owners had hired contractors to salvage the ship, but the tide of fortune was with Midgett. When said and done, he received a check for $4,600, which he and some cohorts earned by acting as guides for Murphy-Pacific inspectors and for transporting them back and forth to the beached ship. The Hatterasers even took soundings around the *Betelgeuse* in preparations for floating it.

Two months after its stranding, the *Betelgeuse* was refloated and towed to Norfolk, where it was inspected for leaks before resuming its trip to Texas. One person who was glad to see the old ship go was Ed Goldberg, who had an interest in the oceanfront development Hatteras Colony at Salvo. According to newspaper accounts, Goldberg claimed that the constant barrage of onlookers left behind litter as well as damaged roads and dunes when taking a look at the stranded vessel. He described the mess left by visitors as "just unbelievable."

TWO FOR THE RECORD BOOKS

Nobody Saw the 1933 Hurricane Season Coming—Which Is Why We Remember It Eighty Years Later

In today's modern age, news crews and satellites keep tabs on a tropical system from the moment it forms to the second it fizzles, but imagine being struck blindly with hurricane force, then getting sucker punched again in a matter of weeks. Such was the case in 1933, when two storms hit the Outer Banks inside of a month.

The first snuck up on the northern beaches on August 23. Elizabeth City's Braxton Dawson left his Nags Head cottage to get some gas and returned to find ocean water lapping at the back door. Advised to leave, locals had to lead Dawson along old sand back roads just to reach the Wright Memorial Bridge, because the Beach Road—only two years old—had washed away in several places. That night, Statesville, North Carolina's the *Landmark* reported that in Nags Head, "Oceanside cottagers flocked to Leroy's Seaside Inn, [where] the Inn's own power plant furnished lights which were kept burning throughout the night. No one slept."

One can hardly fathom what it was like aboard the *G.A. Kohler*. With the four-masted schooner moored off of Chicamacomico, the hurricane's ninety-mile-per-hour winds dragged it and its two anchors just to the north of Avon. Once the weather subsided, surfmen from the Chicamacomico and Gull Shoals Coast Guard Stations used a Lyle gun (an apparatus used to fire a rope to a vessel in distress) to shoot a line to the ship and, with the help of a breeches buoy, rescued eight crew members and the captain's wife. The ship ended up on the beach, where it became an iconic symbol of the Graveyard of the Atlantic and made big news inland. But, as the *Landmark*

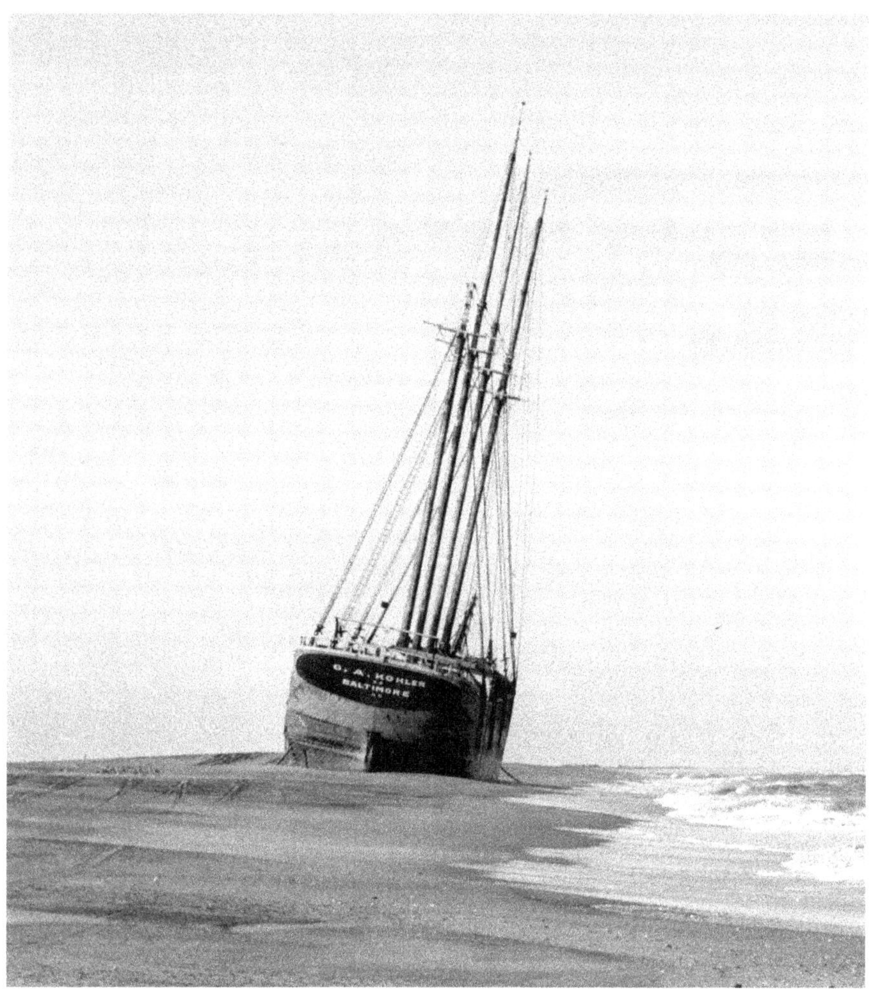

The four-masted schooner *G.A. Kohler* beached high and dry on Hatteras Island. *National Park Service Photo Collection, 1933.*

further noted, "snatching seafarers from the wrath of the Atlantic is all in the day's work for these hardy lifesavers who man the coast guard stations on a desolate shore dreaded by all mariners."

Barely three weeks later, they'd be working overtime when a second storm passed over the Outer Banks on September 16. The *Danville Bee* printed that in Rodanthe, "High seas swept through houses for three days and surfman M.L. O'Neal and Fred O'Neal...were injured during the long fight to prevent loss of life."

Meanwhile, the crew of the Bodie Island Coast Guard Station retreated to the safety of the nearby lighthouse after the station's foundation was undermined by encroaching waves. Maxie Berry, of Pea Island Station's famous all-black crew, left his home on Roanoke Island with his fourteen-year-old son, Zion. They were in a twenty-four-foot boat on route to Pea Island when the storm hit. The pair managed to keep the vessel afloat and washed ashore near Rodanthe, where they took shelter at the home of Zene Midgett.

Out at sea, the luxury passenger ship *Morro Castle*—bound for New York from Havana—was incapacitated off Cape Hatteras. When water began to creep into passengers' cabins, cruisers assembled in the ship's lounge. With the orchestra seasick, twenty-two-year-old Gwendolyn Taylor of Philadelphia, a pretty blonde songstress, took it upon herself to entertain her shipmates and distract them from their perilous situation by playing the piano and singing for hours. "I played and sang cheerful things," she later told reporters. "I think some of the women wanted to hear hymns, but I thought they needed jazz more."

It would be some time before Outer Bankers felt like dancing. When the weather cleared, a new inlet had formed on Hatteras Island near the Creed's Hill Life-Saving Station; another broke through north of Kitty Hawk. A breach in the Manteo–Nags Head Causeway separated Roanoke Island from the beaches. Manteo's Dare County Courthouse suffered enough damage in the roof and cupola (which was later removed) that water funneled into the building. And on Hatteras Island, fishermen lost nets, fish houses, icehouses and homes, leaving them with no or little means of making a living.

Still, with just one drowning casualty, the human toll on the Outer Banks was minimal compared to coastal communities farther south. Down in Carteret County, houses collapsed or were washed away, leaving families to cling to the wreckage and to one another. The community of Merrimon reported that the water rose sixteen feet. Children were swept from their parents' arms. Some families rode out the storm on rooftops, the only points remaining above the tide.

All told, twenty-one people lost their lives in North Carolina, and over one thousand buildings were destroyed, making the September storm among the state's deadliest ever. When the water receded, the 1933 hurricane season left an indelible mark.

THE WRECK OF THE *HELEN H. BENEDICT*

The Details Are in the Documents

Tales of shipwrecks are part of the lore that makes the Outer Banks special. Its formidable spot, jutting out into the great Atlantic, and the dynamics of the flow of the Gulf Stream and remnants of the Labrador Current near Cape Hatteras, make for tricky navigation. Hundreds of vessels have run afoul along the North Carolina coast, and many are documented in the official records of the U.S. Life-Saving Service, and later, the U.S. Coast Guard.

Beginning in the 1870s, lifesaving stations of the recently federally mandated United States Life-Saving Service, were established up and down the coast and were usually manned by a crew of six men and a keeper, whose job it was to patrol the beaches to protect lives and shipping interests. Each time assistance was rendered, the keeper of the station filled out a lengthy form called a wreck report to document which ship was given aid, how many people were saved or lost, the time of the rescue, the conditions of the air and sea at the time of discovery, who reported the vessel in distress and other pertinent information. These records are valuable tools in understanding our maritime past when great sloops and schooners traveled from ports as far away as South America, bringing goods to the maritime centers of the East Coast—Boston, New Haven, New York, Baltimore, Norfolk, Charleston and Jacksonville, to name a few.

But during the great seafaring voyages, foul weather or other vexations could cause a vessel to run aground between ports. Sometimes ships would remain intact, but at other times they bore the brunt of the sea and after grounding in the shallows within sight of shore, broke up after the incessant pounding of the ocean waves.

Shipwrecks often occurred in sparsely settled areas of the coast, and many took place without ever having a mention made in any local newspapers, especially if the ship hailed from a far-off port. Such was the case of the *Helen H. Benedict.*

The three-masted schooner (built circa 1880) from New Haven, Connecticut, was sailing south from Perth Amboy, New Jersey, to Fernandina Beach, Florida, with a captain and a crew of six when it ran into high seas and thick foggy weather. It stranded eighty yards off the beach at Nags Head, North Carolina, on February 6, 1914.

The unfortunate grounding took place at 5:30 a.m. two and a half miles south southeast of the Nags Head Life-Saving Station, which was located oceanfront in the vicinity of where Nags Head Town Hall stands today. At 5:45 a.m., the *Helen H. Benedict* was discovered by James E. Gray, surfman number 6 at the Nags Head Station, who spotted the wreck on his morning patrol and reported it back at the station.

Van Buren Etheridge, veteran keeper of the Nags Head station, telephoned captain J.T. Etheridge of the Bodie Island Life-Saving Station just over seven miles to the south, "requesting him to come with his crew and lend us such assistance as the occasion demanded." The Nags Head crew left at 6:10 a.m. and arrived at the scene of the wreck at 6:45 a.m. and began the process of the rescue.

Because the sea was too rough to launch a surfboat, a breeches buoy was used to rescue Captain Torrey and the crew of the *Helen H. Benedict.* Imagine this contraption as a life-ring with a canvas seat. It was pulled out to the ship via a system of ropes and pulleys. Those on board the distressed ship would one by one get in the seat (which had holes in it to let your legs hang free) to be hauled back to shore above the waves and heavy surf.

In order to get a line to out to the *Helen H. Benedict,* a shot was discharged by the Lyle gun. In a case of extreme danger when lives were at risk, it was important to make the connection with the ship as quickly as possible. If the shot from the Lyle gun did not have enough power, it wouldn't reach the ship, but if the shot had too much power, the line would be propelled over the ship. Once the rope reached the stranded vessel, it was then secured by someone on board if he was capable.

But during the combined life-saving crews' attempt to remove passengers from the *Helen H. Benedict,* a strange thing happened; the passengers stayed on board. Captain Etheridge reported:

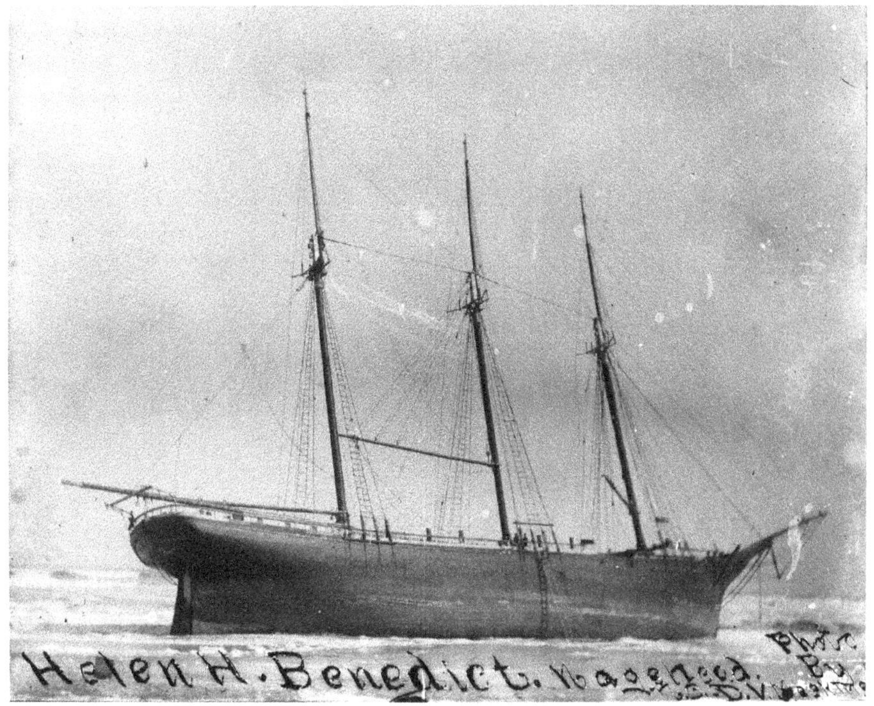

The three-masted schooner *Helen H. Benedict* aground at Nags Head. *D. Victor Meekins Glass Plate Negative Collection, Outer Banks History Center, 1914.*

> *I noticed that no one of the ship's crew attempted to leave the ship, then surfman George T. Wescott was hauled off in the breeches buoy to ascertain the cause of the delay. While on board of ship surfman Wescott aided the crew in preparing their belongings for transferring to the beach. This being done, then we landed surfman Wescott and the entire crew of seven men with the breeches buoy with out any mishaps whatsoever.*

According to the wreck report, the breeches buoy was retrieved twenty times in all to unload the passengers and their baggage. The surfmen and ship's crew returned to the station at noon.

The cook and four seamen from the *Helen H. Benedict* stayed on at the Nags Head station five days, while the captain and the mate stayed for seventeen days, and between them all ate 177 meals. The owner of the *Helen H. Benedict* saved the foresail and the yawl, and although the estimated value of the vessel was $8,000, it was sold "as she lay" for $450. The graceful ship was just one of the many victims of the Graveyard of the Atlantic.

ICEBOUND

The Winter of 1918

A century ago, the new year dawned frigid. As December 1917 came to a close, a tsunami of a cold wave brought temperatures so low that frozen sounds trapped boats in place. Water transportation, the only means of accessing the islands and peninsulas at that time, came to a halt. Food supplies dwindled. Pile on a snowstorm and a freak winter hurricane with winds clocked at seventy-four miles per hour, and you've got a serious winter of discontent.

On January 2, 1918, Manteo's mayor, B.G. Crisp, captured the quick-freeze in a letter to North Carolina supreme court chief justice Walter Clark: "As I write it is snowing, having continuously done so since early morning, it now being about 10 p.m. All the sounds are frozen over. Parties have walked to and from Nags Head during the day. The regular Elizabeth City boat is aground and ice locked about two miles from the north end of Roanoke Island where she has been since Saturday night." However, the storm delayed mail service, so Crisp's letter would not reach its Raleigh recipient for over two weeks. Meanwhile, more boats would fall victim.

The U.S. Coast and Geodetic Survey schooner *Matchless*—temporarily based in Manteo while surveying the Croatan and Roanoke Sounds—was one of the first ships caught in the storm's icy grasp. According to the USC&GS *Annual Report for 1918*, the crew had completed its assigned tasks on December 27 and was prepared to sail to Pasquotank County for repairs and maintenance, when "followed a series of gales and snow with freezing weather, and the vessel was held in the ice until January 17 when the ice was broken up and the schooner was towed to Elizabeth City."

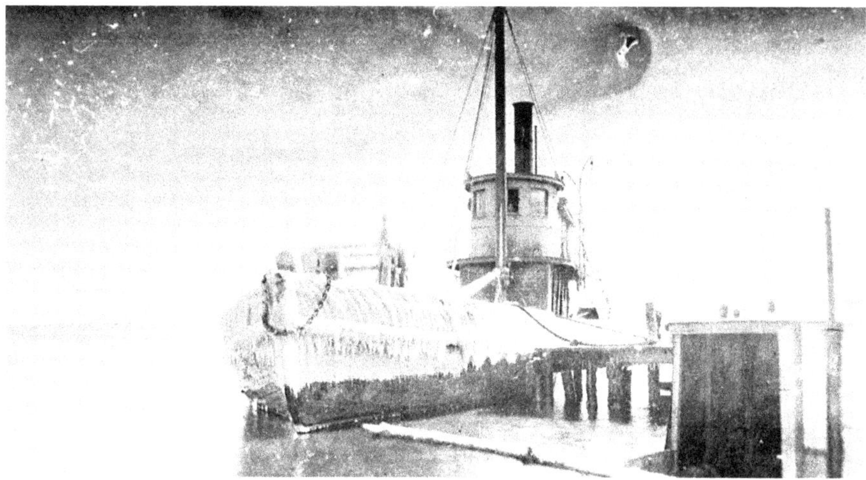

Boats were frozen in place during the big freeze of January 1918. Water travel to the Outer Banks was stymied, and provisions began to dwindle. *Charles Evans Collection, Outer Banks History Center, circa 1918.*

On January 3, C.W. Pugh—keeper at the Roanoke Marshes lighthouse in the lower Croatan Sound off of Wanchese—had to help the steamer *E.R. Daniels* out of the ice and tow the vessel to Manteo. But in a strange case of rescuer becoming rescued, eight days later on January 11, Navy reservist William B. Gray carried provisions out to the lighthouse by means of a fishing dory turned ice craft. Gray adhered runners to the bottom of the fishing boat and was then able to slide on the ice out to the screw-pile light. The Hatteras Island native later earned a commendation from Secretary of the Navy, and fellow North Carolinian, Josephus B. Daniels. Pugh also received recognition from the Lighthouse Service for remaining at his post during the cold storm and for his "loyal devotion to duty under hazardous conditions."

Adding further misery to an already bleak situation, on January 15, a blustery storm—described as a "hurricane" in newspaper accounts—swept over the sandbanks, blowing sixteen homes from their foundations and destroying four altogether. Twelve islanders were injured, and fisherman Monroe Willis perished when he was trapped in the cabin of an overturned boat.

After the gale, fifty citizens attempted to flee Roanoke Island aboard the steamer *E.R. Daniels*, but the ship was forced ashore at Moyock because of heavy ice on the sound. Others boarded the *Hattie Creef* in hopes of reaching the mainland, but the small vessel was no match for the frozen waters.

Fortunately, thawing temperatures were quick to follow. By January 19, it was reported that in Elizabeth City, "Boats from Roanoke Island, Hatteras, Nags Head, Columbia, East Lake, Buffalo and other ports are coming in and going out loaded with provisions to carry back home for the first time in almost three weeks."

They arrived just in time. According to contemporary reports, "The stocks of groceries and other food stuffs in the small stores were exhausted several days ago and the people have been forced to divide among themselves what little food they had at their homes. Had the icebound conditions in the sound continued for more days, it is certain there would have been untold suffering and possibly many deaths."

Perhaps the writer from the *Charlotte Observer* summed up the ordeal best when he said, "The life of these islanders is a lonely and unenviable one under the best of circumstances. Under conditions that have prevailed the last few days it is one of actual terror."

SELECT BIBLIOGRAPHY

Aerial Age Weekly. "Regular Airmail Service to Cuba Now in Operation." December 6, 1920: 342.

Allaback, Sarah. *Mission 66 Visitor Centers: The History of a Building Type.* Washington, D.C.: National Park Service, 2000.

Annual Report of the Superintendent of the US Coast and Geodetic Survey for the Fiscal Year Ending June 30, 1918. Washington, DC: Government Printing Office.

Annual Report of the United States Coast Guard for the Fiscal Year Ended June 30, 1921. Washington, DC: Government Printing Office.

Avalon Beach promotional brochure, circa 1950. Outer Banks History Center, Manteo, NC.

Bakersfield Californian. "Scientist Creates New Type of Kite." May 11, 1953: 17.

Barnes, Jay. *North Carolina's Hurricane History.* Chapel Hill: University of North Carolina Press, 1998.

Basnight, Cora Mae, Suzanne Tate and James Melvin. *Memories of Manteo and Roanoke Island, N.C.* Nags Head, NC: Nags Head Art, ca. 1988.

Beaufort (NC) News. "Catharine of Carteret Christens Cabin Cruiser Croatan with Clam Juice." March 23, 1939: 1.

Bell, Heywood. "Hatteras Hit Hard by Gale Starts Anew." *Danville (VA) Bee,* September 19, 1933: 5.

Binkley, Cameron. *The Creation and Establishment of Cape Hatteras National Seashore: The Great Depression through Mission 66.* Atlanta, GA: Cultural Resources Division, Southeast Regional Office, National Park Service, 2007.

Binkley, Cameron, and Steven A. Davis. *Preserving the Mystery: An Administrative History of Fort Raleigh National Historic Site*. Atlanta, GA: Cultural Resources, Southeast Region, National Park Service, 2003.

Broughton, J. Melville. "To R.R. Waesche." August 27, 1941. State Archives of North Carolina Department of Conservation and Development, Administrative Reports and Correspondence. Box 6.

Burlington (NC) Daily Times News. "Vigil for Ship Not Worthwhile." January 30, 1976: 2B.

Cantaluppi, Carl. "Sweet Potato History: Did You Know?" North Carolina Cooperative Extension Service. Accessed June 17, 2016. https://granville.ces.ncsu.edu/2013/09/sweet-potato-history-did-you-know-2.

Coastland Times (Manteo, NC). "Bids of $951,000 Received for New U.S. 158 Project." June 28, 1957: 1.

———. "Bypass Name to Be Chosen by Contest." March 8, 1983: 1.

———. "Celebrates Birthday with Beach Party." October 19, 1956: 7.

———. "Dedicate Bridge for Manteo's Own Cora Mae." June 17, 1984: 5A.

———. "Exotic Snails Slow to Disappear from KDH." June 22, 1999: 1.

———. "Federal Mackerel Rules Set." September 17, 1991: 1.

———. "Held Secret of Unusual Skill." November 11, 1976: 9B.

———. "High Rise Comes to Dare Coast in 1968 Building." December 29, 1967: 1.

———. "Interest Pays Off." February 12, 1976: 1.

———. "James E. Wood to Sign Books Saturday, July 11 in Manteo." July 9, 1992: 13.

———. Letter to the editor. February 25, 1971: 4.

———. "May Lose $700,000 Highway Proposed on Dare Beaches." November 2, 1956: 1.

———. "Minimum Speed for 158 Urged." August 10, 1962: 1.

———. "More Dope Floats Up on Beaches." October 25, 1979: 1.

———. "Nags Head Discusses Markers." September 9, 1980: 1.

———. "Sawfish Bill Relic of the Deep Still Missing." August 1, 1969: 2.

———. "Seven 1st Ladies Are Honored at Colony Program." July 27, 1962: 5.

———. "Strange Return of Sawfish Bill Noted." August 22, 1969: 4.

———. "Strikingly Different Hotel Opening Saturday at Kitty Hawk Beach." June 29, 1951: 1.

———. "Summer Cottages Sprouting Like Flowers in Early Spring." March 27, 1953: 2.

———. "They Enjoyed Indoor Swimming Pool." April 19, 1973: 9.

———. "This Was the Scene on Friday." March 16, 1976: 1.

———. "Three Days of Commemoration Events Thrill Crowds at Manteo." June 17,1984: 1.

———. "What Would You Do with It?" February 17, 1976: 5.

Crumley, Brian T., and Frank J.J. Miele. *Roanoke Island, 1865–1940, Special History Study.* Atlanta, GA: Cultural Resources Division, Southeast Regional Office, National Park Service, 2005. Accessed June 16, 2018. http://purl.access.gpo.gov/GPO/LPS115692.

Cumo, Christopher. *Science and Technology in 20th-Century American Life.* Westport, CT: Greenwood Press, 2007.

Currituck County. February 2014. *Corolla Village Circulation and Wayfinding Plan.*

Daily Advance (Elizabeth City, NC). "Captain Martin L. Johnson Is Veteran Sailor of Dare Water Routes and Bypaths." November 18, 1932.

———. "Mile Signs Posts Will Be Erected on Dare Beaches." March 20, 1950: 8.

Daily Press (Hampton, VA). Francis M. Rogallo, September 6, 2009.

Daily Tar Heel (Chapel Hill, NC). "Federal Project Will Create Roanoke Island Acting Group." February 20, 1936: 1.

Damerow, Gail. "Escargot From Your Own Backyard." *Mother Earth News,* June/July 1993.

Davis, Susan Joy. *The Whalehead Club: Reflections of Currituck Heritage.* Virginia Beach: Donning Company, 2004.

Dean, Earl. "The Steamer Trenton Recalled by Aging Master in Manteo." *Coastland Times,* March 18, 1955: 1.

Eaton, Lorraine. Interview by author, June 10, 2016.

———. "Odd Lodgings: A Survey of Offbeat Outer Banks Beach Rentals." *Carolina Coast,* June 25, 1991.

———. "Rotten Raleigh: Manteo to Behead Sir Walter." *Virginian-Pilot,* April 7, 1989: Section A.

Farmer and Mechanic (Raleigh, NC). "Growing Cranberries in North Carolina." December 31, 1907: 3.

Figuier, Louis, and Charles O. Groom-Napier. *The Ocean World: Being a Description of the Sea, and Its Living Inhabitants.* London: Chapman & Hall, 1869.

Free Lance-Star (Fredericksburg, VA). "Virginia Landfall for Smuggling." October 1, 1976: 13.

Gastonia (NC) Gazette. "Ocean Has Strange Inhabitants." July 9, 1949: 16.

Hacker, Barton C., and James M. Grimwood. *On the Shoulders of Titans: A History of Project Gemini.* 2003. Accessed April 14, 2018. http://www.hq.nasa.gov/office/pao/History/SP-4203/cover.htm.

High Point (NC) Enterprise. "Hatteras Meeting Convenes." August 25, 1941: 3.

Independent (Elizabeth City, NC). "Balboa Caught Fire at Manteo." December 31, 1920: 1.

———. "A Big Help to Roanoke Island." November 19, 1920: 5.

———. "Captain Martin Johnson Loses Mail Contract." February 26, 1932: 5.

———. "Famous Elizabeth City Girl to Develop Elizabethan Play Group on Roanoke Island." February 16, 1934: 2.

———. "Ferry Service from This City to Manteo." November 11, 1927: 3.

———. "First Cuban Mail Planes Land at Roanoke Island." October 29, 1920: 1.

———. "Grows Sweet Potato Nearly a Yard Long." November 21, 1919: 1.

———. "Has Sailed a Million and Quarter Miles." July 1, 1932: Section 2, 3.

———. "Is Manteo Hoodoo Port for Cuban Mail Planes." February 25, 1921: 1.

———. "Kitty Hawk Transients Expect to Preserve Dare Co.'s Coastal Wonderland." June 8, 1934: 3.

———. "Not a Mishap in a Million Miles." August 13, 1926: Section 2, 1.

———. "Storm Damage to Dare County May Never Be Figured Out." September 22, 1933: 2.

———. "This May be the Doom of S.S. Trenton." November 27, 1931: 1.

———. "Worst Storm in City's History." August 25, 1933: 4.

Jones, Morgan. "The Naturalist's Notebook: Dinosaurs in the Rivers?" *Coastwatch Magazine*, Spring 2013.

Jordan, Ida Kay. "Currituck Mourns Famed Goose-Caller." *Virginian-Pilot*, April 3, 1990: D1.

Khoury, Angel Ellis. *Manteo: A Roanoke Island Town*. Virginia Beach: Donning Company, 1999.

LeDoux, Julia. "President Joins Celebration." *Outer Banks Sentinel*, December 19, 2003: 1.

Ludbell, David. "Are Land Snails a Signature for the Mesolithic-Neolithic Transition?" *Documenta Praehistorica XXXI,* 2004.

MacNeill, Ben Dixon. "MacNeill Uncovers Hayman Potato Story in Old Book Kept by Hatteras Mariner." *Coastland Times*, December 17, 1954: 1.

Maddry, Lawrence. "Champion Caller Bill Privott Is a Man Who Usually Gets His Goose." *Sports Illustrated*, February 11, 1985. Accessed January 29, 2018. https://www.si.com/vault/1985/02/11/628418/champion-caller-bill-privott-is-a-man-who-usually-gets-his-goose.

———. "A Voice of Dissent on the Outer Banks." *Coastland Times*, September 28, 1962: 1.

McKee, Brent. Interview by author, April 30, 2018.

Midgette, Lynda. Interview by author, May 2007.

Monroe (NC) Journal. "Cape Hatteras Struck by Hurricane." January 18, 1918: 6.

Moore, Cecelia. *The Federal Theatre Project in the American South: The Carolina Playmakers and the Quest for American Drama*. Lanham, MD: Lexington Books, 2017.

Morrill, Dan. "No Daub, No Wattles: Coquina Beach at Nags Head to Feature Modern Trend in Architectural Ideas." *Virginian-Pilot,* July 22, 1956.

Morris, James H. "Corolla and the Space Age." *Daily Times-News* (Burlington, NC). Three-part series for the Associated Press, August 1–3, 1962.

Morris, Travis. *Untold Stories of Old Currituck Duck Clubs*. Charleston, SC: The History Press, 2010.

National Register of Historic Places, Nags Head Beach Cottages Historic District, Nags Head, North Carolina, National Register #77000997.

News and Observer (Raleigh, NC). "Sixteen Days from Manteo to Raleigh." January 19, 1918: 5.

———. "Water Transportation Is Being Resumed." January 20, 1918: 1.

New York Times. "F.M. Rogallo, 97, Father of Hang Gliding." September 4, 2009: D8.

———. "President Shooting Snipe." May 22, 1894.

North Carolina Department of Agriculture and Consumer Services, Plant Industry Division. *2011–2012 Fiscal Year Report.*

North Carolina Department of Conservation and Development. *Biennial Report for the Year Ending June 30, 1940.*

North Carolina Emergency Relief Administration, J.S. Kirk, W.A. Cutter, and Thomas W. Morse. *Emergency Relief in North Carolina: A Record of the Development and the Activities of the North Carolina Emergency Relief Administration, 1932–1935. North Carolina Emergency Relief Commission, State Administrator, Mrs. Thomas O'Berry*. Raleigh: Edwards & Broughton, 1936.

Outlaw, Edward Ralph. *Old Nag's Head: Personal Recollections and Some History of the Region in North Carolina at the Edge of the Sea Where Our First Colonists Landed*. Norfolk, VA: Liskey Lithograph Corp., 1956.

Pearce, David. Interview by author, 2014.

Powell, William Stevens, and Michael R. Hill. *The North Carolina Gazetteer: A Dictionary of Tar Heel Places and Their History: The Classic Reference Updated for a New Generation, with More than 20,000 Entries*. Chapel Hill: University of North Carolina Press, 2010.

———. *North Carolina through Four Centuries*. Chapel Hill: University of North Carolina Press, 1990.

———. *Paradise Preserved*. Chapel Hill: University of North Carolina Press, 1965.

Price, Robert Henderson. *Sweet Potato Culture for Profit. A Full Account of the Origin, History and Botanical Characteristics of the Sweet Potato*. Dallas: Texas Farm and Ranch, 1896.

Privott, Bill. Interview by author, May 12, 2018, June 18, 2018.

Reports of the Department of Commerce, 1918. Washington, D.C.: Government Printing Office.

Rich, Brad, "Protecting the Sturgeon: Joy and Consternation." *Coastal Review Online*, April 4, 2012, Accessed April 22, 2018, https://www.coastalreview.org/2012/04/protecting-the-sturgeon-joy-and-consternation.

Richmond Times-Dispatch. "Relief Reaches People on Islands off Coast." January 17, 1918: 9.

Roanoke Beacon (Plymouth, NC). "List of Awards for Horticulture Exhibits at the Jamestown Exposition." January 24, 1908: 8.

Robesonian (Lumberton, NC). "Irish Ambassador to Visit Birthplace of Irish Potato." May 21, 1953: 3.

Rocky Mount (NC) Evening Telegram. "Giant Sawfish Caught." July 20, 1951: 2B.

Rocky Mount (NC) Sunday Telegram. "Wild Cranberries Being Harvested in Abundance in Bogs of Dare Co.." November 25, 1951: 10B.

Rountree, Susan Byrum. *Nags Headers*. Winston-Salem, NC: John F. Blair, 2001.

Semi-weekly Messenger (Wilmington, NC). "Eastern Carolina Cranberries." November 15, 1901: 5.

Senter, Jim. "Live Dunes and Ghost Forests: Stability and Change in the History of North Carolina's Maritime Forests." *North Carolina Historical Review* 80, 3 (July 2003): 334–71.

Smith, Hugh M. *The Fishes of North Carolina*. Raleigh: E.M. Uzzell, state printers and binders, 1907.

Spence, George. "My Boyhood at the Beach." Unpublished manuscript at the Outer Banks History Center, 2013.

Statesville (NC) Record and Landmark. "Hardy Folks Save Ship's Occupants from Death at Sea." August 29, 1933: 7.

———. "Manteo Is Connected with Outside Again." August 29, 1933: 7.

———. "Rocket Facility Planned for State." April 24, 1962: 1.

———. "Ship Rides Out Storm While Woman Plays." September 22, 1933: 3.

Stewart, Arnold J. "Ducky." "Fishing and Hunting." *Wilmington (DE) Morning News*, August 15, 1941.

Stick, David. "Dare Beaches Chamber of Commerce 1947–1950." Unpublished manuscript, Outer Banks History Center, circa 1992.

———. *The Outer Banks of North Carolina, 1584–1958*. Chapel Hill: University of North Carolina Press, 1958.

Toledo Blade. "More Hash Found along Coast." October 22, 1979: 4.

Turek, Eve. Interview by author, May 31, 2017.

Twiddy, Mary Alice. Interview by author, September 9, 2017.

United States Bureau of the Census. Census of Population, 1860. *Currituck County, North Banks District.*

United States Life-Saving Service Wreck Report, Helen H. Benedict, 33MSS-8, Box 5 Folder 54, Outer Banks History Center.

Ward, Alvah H., and R. Wayne Gray. *When Ice Came to the Outer Banks: A Local History of Ice and Its Impact on the Development of the Coastal Region*. N.p., 2013.

Watson, Max. *The Man Who Made Pan Am*. 2015. https://www.overdrive.com/search?q=D191E70E-E460-4FE3-B5B4-ADAED2E07973.

Winslow, Cecelia Winslow. Interview by author, January 20, 2018.

Wood, Angel. "To France for Culinary Treats." *Coastland Times*, January 15, 1981: B1.

Young, Tanya. Interview by author, March 24, 2014.

ABOUT THE AUTHOR

Sarah Downing loves to share stories about the Outer Banks. She lived there for thirty years and was immersed in the history and culture of the barrier islands, especially in her role as assistant curator of the Outer Banks History Center and as a freelance writer. Downing now writes in the shadow of the Blue Ridge Mountains from her home outside of Asheville, North Carolina. She enjoys dancing, hiking, swimming, cooking and eating ice cream. She lives with her husband of thirty-plus years and a mixed breed dog. *Chronicles of the Outer Banks: Fish Tales and Salty Gales* is her sixth book.

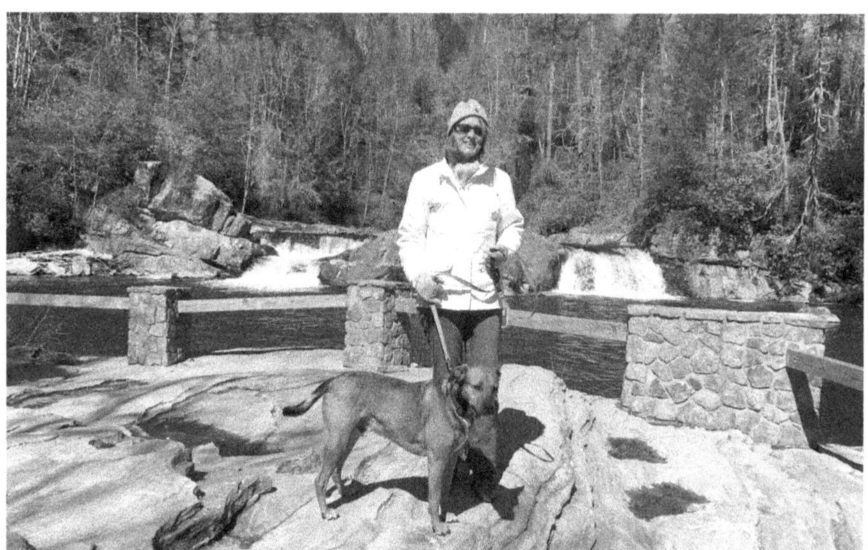

www.ingramcontent.com/pod-product-compliance
Lightning Source LLC
LaVergne TN
LVHW052337100826
845147LV00020B/1097

* 9 7 8 1 4 6 7 1 4 0 9 1 1 *